REVITALIZING CITIES

H. Briavel Holcomb
Department of Urban Studies

and

Robert A. Beauregard
Department of Urban Planning and Policy Development

School of Urban and Regional Policy
Rutgers University
New Brunswick, New Jersey

RESOURCE PUBLICATIONS
IN GEOGRAPHY

Library of Congress Card Number 81-69237
ISBN 0-89291-148-4

Library of Congress Cataloging in Publication Data

Holcomb, H. Briavel.
  Revitalizing cities.

  (Resouce publications in geography)
  Bibliography: p.
  1. Urban renewal — United States. 2. Cities and towns
— United States. 3. Urban renewal — Canada. 4. Cities
and towns — Canada. I. Beauregard, Robert A. II. Title.
III. Series.
HT175.H64   307'.34'0973   81-69237
ISBN 0-89291-148-4   AACR2

Publication Supported by the A.A.G.

Graphic Design by D. Sue Jones and CGK

Printed by Commercial Printing Inc.
State College, Pennsylvania

Cover Photograph: Montreal, Courtesy of Charles I. Siegel

Foreword

The 1980 Census of Population indicates that 18 percent of the American population lives in the central cities of our fifty largest metropolitan areas; 45 percent reside within the metropolitan areas of these cities. Another 30 percent reside in the 268 smaller, designated metropolitan areas of the nation. Although the non-metropolitan population is now fastest-growing, and central city decline continues in the Northeast and North Central regions, it is erroneous to suggest, as did President Carter's Commission for a National Agenda for the Eighties, that central city decline is inevitable, let alone desirable or tolerable. Many forms of urban revitalization belie a notion of the city destined to death — redeveloped central business districts, boutiqued Main Streets, and gentrified neighborhoods. Why is revitalization occurring? What is its extent? What are its consequences and prospects? These are the questions addressed by Briavel Holcomb and Robert A. Beauregard in *Revitalizing Cities*.

The title of this book connotes two major goals. First, *Revitalizing Cities* describes urban areas in which symptoms of decline — disinvestment, population loss, deterioration — are being slowed or reversed. In this sense, we learn about projects, public and private, corporate and personal, that may alter the trajectory of recent urban change. Second, *Revitalizing Cities* discusses the process of revitalization — actors, intentions, plans, and construction — focusing on the need for ameliorating the unfortunate, negative consequences of urban redevelopment sustained by the displaced.

Few Americans would see a parallel between the urban spatial structures of South Africa's *apartheid* system and their own cities. Yet, the relocations of blacks and coloreds in order to achieve racial separation in South Africa has a striking parallel in American gentrification. As reviewer Joseph Lelyveld wrote in his review of John Western's *Outcast Cape Town*:

> For his next study, [Western] might consider comparing the Cape Town experience to the renovation of landmark neighborhoods in one of our Eastern cities. When he talks of the destruction of community feeling and the criminal cultures that have been bred on the remote Cape flats, . . . the comparison seems uncomfortably close.*

Geography, among other sciences, incorporates several alternative perspectives, fundamental beliefs about the kinds of questions asked and the approaches used. A critical understanding of revitalization may be derived from several viewpoints discussed by Holcomb and Beauregard. The authors' primary concern with justice and equity will be shared by many readers, who may be motivated by moral, philosophical, analytical, or practical imperatives.

Resource Publications in Geography are sponsored by the Association of American Geographers, a professional organization whose purpose is to advance studies in geography and to encourage the application of geographic research in education, government, and business. This series traces its origins to the Association's

---

*J. Western, *Outcast Cape Town* (Minneapolis: University of Minnesota Press, 1981), reviewed by J. Lelyveld, "The Designs of Apartheid," *New York Times Book Review*, January 24, 1982, quotation from p. 16.

Commission on College Geography, whose *Resource Papers* were launched in 1968. Eventually 28 papers were published under sponsorship of the Commission through 1974 with the assistance of the National Science Foundation. Continued NSF support after completion of the Commission's work permitted the *Resource Papers for College Geography* to meet the original series goals for an additional four years and sixteen volumes:

> *The Resource Papers have been developed as expository documents for the use of both the student and the instructor. They are experimental in that they are designed to supplement existing texts and to fill a gap between significant research in American geography and readily accessible materials. The papers are concerned with important concepts or topics in modern geography and focus on one of three general themes: geographic theory, policy implications, or contemporary social relevance. They are designed to implement a variety of undergraduate college geography courses at the introductory and advanced level.*

The popularity and usefulness of the two series suggested the importance of their continuation after 1978, once a self-supporting basis for their publication had been established.

For the **Resource Publications,** the original goals remain paramount. However, they have been broadened to include the continuing education of professional geographers as well as communication with the public on contemporary issues of geographic relevance. This monograph was developed, printed and distributed under the auspices of the Association, whose members served in advisory and review roles during its preparation. The ideas presented, however, are the authors' and do not imply AAG endorsement.

We hope that this book conveys some of the vitality of urban revitalization. Redeveloped parts of cities are exciting places to see, visit, experience, and, for many, to live. A recent survey of urban quality-of-life** tells us what residents have said for a long time: the Pittsburghs and Philadelphias may not have the glamour of the Sunbelt's Houston or Phoenix, but they remain good, if not better, places to live. When we experience the positive results of urban revitalization, we will also be aware of the costs sustained by displaced businesses and residents, of their exploitation. For students, we intend that this book will generate an understanding of urban dynamics in the 1980's. For colleagues, this work provides a summary of current programs and a geographical exploration of revitalization's causes and consequences. For professional urban planners and city leaders, this book is intended to provide encouragement, yet awareness of unfulfilled needs that must be addressed as revitalization progresses.

C. Gregory Knight
The Pennsylvania State University
Editor, Resource Publications in Geography

Resource Publications Advisory Board

George, W. Carey, *Rutgers University*
James S. Gardner, *University of Waterloo*
Charles M. Good, Jr., *Virginia Polytechnic Institute and State University*
Mark S. Monmonier, *Syracuse University*
Risa I. Palm, *University of Colorado*
Thomas J. Wilbanks, *Oak Ridge National Laboratories*

**R. Boyer and D. Savageau, *Places Rated Almanac* (Chicago: Rand McNally, 1981).

Preface and Acknowledgements

It is difficult to live in the northeastern United States and be unaware of its vulnerable economic base, lagging population growth, and deteriorating cities. For those who reside in old industrial cities, decline and its consequences are particularly striking. No less evident is the hope that many have for urban revitalization. The excitement and vibrancy of a dense and diverse urban environment is still cherished by many people who live in and frequent central cities. The attraction of urban living and concern for those who bear the burden of urban decline led us to explore the process of urban revitalization, its consequences, and the attendant ideology of dreams and deceptions.

Although there is a burgeoning literature on urban revitalization, there is still need for an overview from a geographic perspective. This work fills that gap within a framework of social justice. Our ideological perspective is skeptical of capitalism and supports economic and social democracy. We introduce the broad dimensions of urban revitalization in such a way as to challenge the reader's critical spirit and to encourage further inquiry.

This work is most suitable as a supplementary text in courses on urban geography, urban studies, urban planning, urban sociology, and political geography for advanced undergraduate and beginning graduate students. With appropriate supplementary readings (many of which are listed in the bibliography), it could serve as the centerpiece of a course on urban redevelopment or as the single text for short seminars and mini-courses. It could be a starting point for academic research and for the involvement of students in community projects. Various simulation games might be devised around investment, taxation and land use conflicts using roles developed to represent government officials, business people, gentrifiers, and poor residents. The background material provided by this work can also be assigned in preparation for debates about controversial recommendations for national, state, or local urban policy.

Although convention requires that one author be listed first, our co-authorship was a truly equal and complementary undertaking. Briavel wrote the initial proposal, but the subsequent writing and logistical details were equally shared.

Of course, no work of this nature is without its many contributors. In addition to those whose writings provided intellectual stimulation, certain of our friends and colleagues willingly gave of their time and mental effort to read and criticize drafts of various chapters. We wish to thank Kent Barnes, Eugenie Birch, Tom Clark, Carol Corden, Norman Fainstein, Amy Lempert, David Ley, and Marvin Waterstone. Rod Erickson read an early draft of the manuscript; his advice was instrumental in our revisions. Cartographic skills were ably supplied by Anne Bonner. Ruth Cousins provided valuable research assistance in the early stages of this project, and Nancy Swan and Barbara Swan furnished expert typing. Special thanks are extended to Greg Knight who guided this work through its various stages and into the completed version which you now hold. His comments, advice, and gentle prodding were invaluable.

Finally (from HBH), thank you to Genevieve for sacrificing what might have been hours of maternal attention.

H. Briavel Holcomb
Robert A. Beauregard

Contents

List of Figures

1

Geographical Aspects of Urban Revitalization

The late Seventies witnessed a resurgence of private investment and government programs directed toward the redevelopment of commercial districts and the renovation of neighborhoods in cities throughout North America. Baltimore's Inner Harbor was rebuilt, and previously dilapidated rowhouses on Federal Hill and in Fells Point were renovated for middle-class residents. In St. Paul, the Lowertown area, once a warehousing, manufacturing and transportation center, is being converted to a commercial and residential 'village.' New commercial investment focused upon historic market structures in Boston, while nearby warehouses on harbor wharves were being transformed into residences. Neighborhoods in Washington were upgraded ('gentrified') to upper-middle-class respectability; in Vancouver the former industrial area of False Creek became the site of new, amenity-rich housing. Charleston's historic preservation continued to capture public enthusiasm, and in Los Angeles major redevelopment is occurring in the Bunker Hill area. These are a few examples of a phenomenon increasingly apparent in North American cities.

The label for these seemingly diverse activities is *urban revitalization,* meaning, literally, to put new life into cities. Although the term has been in use in the United States since the Thirties, it was not popularized until the Seventies. Like earlier labels (e.g., *urban redevelopment* and *urban renewal),* urban revitalization implies growth, progress, and the infusion of new activities into stagnant or declining cities which are no longer attractive to investors and middle-class households.[1] Typically, urban revitalization involves investment to remodel or rebuild a portion of the urban environment to accommodate more profitable activities and expanded opportunities for consumption, particularly retail and housing for middle- and upper-income households. Succinctly stated, areas of the city are upgraded for "higher" social and economic uses, those activities which generate the greatest profits based on location.

Initially, new private and public investment in cities was enthusiastically heralded and encouraged by local and national communication media. After three decades of stories reporting the deterioration, riots, crime, abandonment, and poverty of the nation's central cities, an abrupt reversal had apparently occurred. Instead of headlines

---

[1]The term 'revitalization' suggests that these cities, or certain parts of them, were lacking any 'life' or were without social usefulness. In many instances, as we will discuss below, revitalized areas of cities, while often deteriorated, did contain working and lower-income households or marginal but operating enterprises employing the working class. They were not 'dead.' See N. Smith (1981).

proclaiming the urban crisis, newspapers and magazines substituted "America Falls in Love With Its Cities — Again" (Sutton 1979), "The Urban Crisis Leaves Town and Moves to the Suburbs" (Allman 1978), "The New Elite and an Urban Renaissance" (Fleetwood 1979), "Downtown is Looking Up" (*Time* 1976), and "Nation's Cities Poised for a Stunning Comeback" (Peirce 1977).

The magnitude and extent of the current revival is debatable, however, and the evidence equivocal. Contradicting the earlier optimistic headlines, the *New York Times* on June 1, July 7, and August 11, 1980, reported " 'Revitalization' Held to be Spotty," "Study Says Old Cities Continue to Decline Despite Rejuvenation," and "The Cities Call Out for Help, But Their Voice is Fainter." Contrary to evidence such as numerous redevelopment projects, renovating neighborhoods, and an increasing rate of household formation, the aggregate statistics of central-city population and employment continued a relentless decline. Even cities with the most conspicuous evidence of revitalization, such as Boston and Baltimore, lost population at a greater rate between 1975 and 1977 than during the decade of the Sixties (Fossett and Nathan 1980). After analyzing available demographic and economic trends in 53 American cities between 1960 and 1977, Fossett and Nathan (1980:5) concluded that "there is little evidence, at least to date, that either residential or economic revitalization has had any appreciable impact on any appreciable number of older cities."

It seems clear that residential and economic revitalization is happening in many, but not all, North American cities. Available data suggest that revitalization is strongest in larger cities and weakest in the West, probably due to the higher proportion of younger cities in that region (Black 1980). While 'Back to the City' is an upbeat slogan, the number of people returning to live in central cities is small compared to the continued outward stream. Gentrifying neighborhoods receive a good deal of publicity, but they are actually few in number and usually small in scale. Many cities show little or no sign of economic revival. Cleveland continues to fight fiscal collapse and staggering losses of population and employment, while nearby Youngstown anticipates trouble following the closure of Youngstown Sheet and Tube (Bluestone *et al.* 1981:22-35). Parts of Camden and Newark, New Jersey, remain vacant or devastated. The overall impact of urban revitalization has not overcome the forces of decline in many cities.

At the same time, some empirical, and much anecdotal, evidence suggests that urban revitalization is localized within cities (Blumenthal 1979). New public and private investments are primarily concentrated in a few desirable neighborhoods and in the major central business district. Lower- and working-class neighborhoods are given only token governmental assistance and are burdened by disinvestment on the part of the private sector. Commercial districts in neighborhoods that are not gentrifying are ignored or provided with minimal assistance. Revitalization creates few worthwhile jobs for lower and working class people, who may face higher rents and displacement as a consequence. Urban revitalization seems exclusionary, both spatially and socially.

Why, then, devote attention to the geography of a relatively small scale, spatially limited, and possibly ephemeral phenomenon? The reasons are several. First, urban revitalization may not be universal, but it does represent a partial reversal of long-term trends upon which previous theories of urban growth and decline have been developed. A thorough explanation of revitalization may require revision of existing urban theory. Second, the present redevelopment could represent the beginning of a longer and more intense trend of urban recovery; on the other hand, it could be transitory, the dying gasp of some cities. Third, the scale of revitalization is relatively small, but the accompanying publicity and rhetoric have created the image of a much larger movement. The image, as we shall see, is important in producing a momentum of progress, instilling confidence in investors. Fourth and most important, urban revitalization generates large profits, but its costs and benefits are unevenly, often inequitably, distributed among socio-economic groups. The urban environment undergoes major modifications, and people's lives are drastically changed.

There are profoundly geographic causes and consequences of urban revitalization. Revitalization is stimulated by the differential profitability of locations, reshaping urban form, modifying the social geography of cities, and bringing new relationships between urban inhabitants and their environment. These issues suggest several underlying geographical dimensions of urban revitalization, providing three important themes. The first and dominant theme is the issue of social justice: the costs and benefits of revitalization are unevenly distributed relative to the needs of various urban groups. The second theme is the impact that urban revitalization has upon urban form, especially in changing land use patterns and creating new landscapes. The third theme is the material and psychological relationships between humans and their environment as modified by redevelopment.

Increasingly, geographers have recognized that the spatial distribution of people, resources, and investment is not neutral in its impact upon the quality of life of various groups within society. This relationship has been established in the literature on social justice (Harvey 1973), welfare approaches to social geography (D. Smith 1977), and theories of dependency and uneven development (Editorial Collective 1978). Underlying a social-justice perspective is the lack of equal access to spatially distributed amenities such as good neighborhoods, investment opportunities, or meaningful employment. Locational decisions which create these distributions are now recognized as insufficiently incorporated in conventional location theory (Cox 1978; Cox 1979).

In urban revitalization, not only are investments unevenly distributed across space, but the costs and benefits generated by these investments disproportionately affect different areas of the city. Uncompensated costs may be unfairly borne by certain groups (such as residents displaced by new construction), while the benefits are often spatially concentrated. This spatial pattern is closely reflected by, and causally linked to, a distribution of costs and benefits by social classes (Peet 1975). Although it is often assumed that the benefits of revitalization will "trickle down" to the lower and working classes in a manner similar to that hypothesized for the housing market (Altshuler 1969; Lowry 1960; W. F. Smith 1971), in fact they are often completely captured by the middle and upper classes. As we explore urban revitalization and the key actors who direct it, the exclusionary nature of revitalization's consequences becomes understandable.

The interpretations of urban landscapes, understanding why particular places are devoted to certain uses and examining the ways in which human values and cultural ideas are reflected in urban habitats, are central concerns of urban geography. The landscape of revitalizing cities is undergoing rapid transformation. Blighted areas are torn down for new office buildings, hotels, theaters, and convention centers. Neighborhood housing stock is transformed from abandoned shells to renovated residences. Commercial districts are developed in newly profitable locations, and old industrial buildings are converted to desirable apartments or shopping malls. Classic theories of urban form inadequately explain the current phenomenon of urban revitalization (Castells 1977:113-242; M. Smith 1979:235-295). They assume a relatively static juxtaposition of land uses or invasion of neighborhoods by different socioeconomic or ethnic groups. These theories fail to account for the role of government and private investors in shaping the built environment for political, economic, and ideological ends (Clark 1980).

As the built environment is transformed, social behavior within that environment undergoes change. Humans actively modify, and adapt to, their environment. Behavioral geographers, environmental psychologists, and others have begun to explore the more subjective issues involved in questions of environmental perception and activity. How do feelings about place influence decisions and behavior (Porteous 1977; Tuan 1977; Tuan 1974)? The image of the revitalizing city, the impression of progress and growth, is considered as critically important by proponents of revitalization. Additionally, attachment to a place (topophilia) can be a powerful force, both in efforts toward preservation and in exacerbating the psychological trauma of relocation (Ford 1974; Fried 1963). Places with symbolic significance to particular groups within society may be preserved and renovated even when economic logic dictates otherwise (Firey 1945).

Our interest in understanding urban revitalization is not only critical but also constructive. We offer suggestions for making revitalization more democratic in process and more egalitarian in consequence. A social-justice perspective and a reexamination of theories of urban form and of changing human-environment relationships in North American cities underlie our discussion of urban revitalization. Our analysis begins with a brief presentation of the historical evolution of urban redevelopment in the United States. Starting with the American Park Movement, various governmental interventions shaped urban redevelopment over the last 130 years. Chapter 2 provides important historical background to the present strategy of urban revitalization. Chapter 3 assesses the spatial extent of and presents various explanations for urban revitalization. Chapters 2 and 3 thus form a prelude to analysis of the geography of urban revitalization as it occurs in commercial districts (Chapter 4) and residential neighborhoods (Chapter 5). In each we examine the components of revitalization and suggest spatial as well as social, economic, and political consequences. Chapter 5 compares gentrifying neighborhoods with those being upgraded without displacement.

Chapter 6 presents a more intensive investigation of the phenomonological aspects of revitalization.[2] Images portrayed by the new built environment, the nostalgia of historic preservation, and feelings of alienation and belonging are central topics. We conclude in Chapter 7 by returning to our three major themes, stressing the importance of a social-justice perspective for understanding and evaluating the process and consequences of urban revitalization. Suggestions for urban policy and political action are offered to make urban revitalization more equitable.

---

[2]Briefly, phenomenologists study the world as subjectively experienced rather than seeking universally accepted notions of objective reality. For further clarification see Gregory (1978) and Relph (1981).

2

Urban Decline and Redevelopment

Urban revitalization is neither completely new nor unprecedented. Cities experience periods of growth and decline, with concomitant transformation of urban space from one economic and social use to another. Not until the late nineteenth and early twentieth centuries, however, did relatively coordinated efforts on the part of local governments, reform groups, and business interests arise with the intent of eliminating the physical manifestation of urban decline (Gelfand 1975:3-22). Over the last 130 years, major efforts have been made in the United States to counteract decay and to rejuvenate cities. These efforts vividly demonstrate that urban form is not a result of natural or inevitable processes. Rather, cities are shaped over time by political, economic, and social forces reflected in organizational and individual decisions. Government is one of the powerful actors in this unfolding drama.

Parks, Civic Centers, and Beautification

The first major redevelopment efforts in the United States were the American Park Movement and the City Beautiful Movement. Each emerged as a response to the high densities and environmental degradation brought about by the conjunction of urbanization and industrialization in the last half of the 19th century and the first two decades of the 20th century.[3] In the industrial city, working class neighborhoods were often highly congested and fire-prone, containing overcrowded tenements with only rudimentary water and sewage services. Industrial districts were adjacent to the newly emerging central business districts and were interspersed with residential neighborhoods, resulting in traffic, air pollution, and constant noise. There were almost no open spaces or parks. The emerging middle class and the rich had homes on the outskirts or in expensive inner-city neighborhoods isolated from squalor and industry. The working class had only the 'gritty city' (Procter and Matuszeski 1978).

Reformers attempted to alleviate slum conditions with health laws and regulations governing tenement construction (Lubove 1962). In the early 1900's cities also experimented with laws governing land use in order to control the location and spread of

---

[3]From 1850 to 1920, the number of cities over 50,000 population grew from 10 to 144; the percentage of population living in urban areas increased from 15.3 to 51.2; and the overall national population multiplied by a factor of five. These and other data in this chapter are from U.S. Bureau of the Census (1975) and U. S. Department of Labor (1976).

undesirable activities (Toll 1969). In turn, reformers and enlightened business interests realized that the existence of slums and the lack of amenities limited investment and constrained the growth of property values.

The American Park Movement can be traced to the 1858 construction of Central Park in New York City. The movement could claim as part of its heritage Fairmount Park in Philadelphia, Prospect Park in Brooklyn, the Fenway Park system in Boston, Golden Gate Park in San Francisco, and a host of other parks in large, industrial cities (Chadwick 1966:166-220; Scott 1969:10-26). Original park proponents were primarily interested in providing recreational space, establishing spatial buffers against the spread of fire and disease, and making an aesthetic contribution to the city. Later, it was realized that parks also increased adjacent land values and could be used to restructure land uses and to eliminate undesirable areas. In most cities, parks were constructed on the urban fringe where land values were low and building demolition was not required. But in some cities, such as Kansas City and New York, park construction entailed the elimination of slums and shanty-towns.

Urban parks were thought to provide city residents with a therapeutic environment. Planners saw passive recreational areas for contemplating nature and fleeing the chaos of the dense industrial city as important for mental well-being (Gans 1968) and moral development (Tuan 1974). The urban park provided an alternative to the ". . . cause-and-effect, finite, scheduled life in a utilitarian, hard-surfaced, busy urban center (Cranz 1978:10). Moreover, parks made new forms of recreation possible and constituted a uniquely urban amenity. By the turn of the century, however, the demand for urban parks had diminished and was replaced by a movement to develop playgrounds for active recreation in working-class neighborhoods.

The City Beautiful Movement evolved from the 1893 World's Columbian Exposition in Chicago. The Exposition site was intended as a prototype for the rebuilding of cities, consisting of a series of monumentally designed buildings, clad in stucco made to look like stone, classically arranged within a landscaped setting of lagoons, boulevards, and majestic open spaces. Within the planned grounds was the Midway Plaisance, an area of commercial and recreational attractions which some interpret as a model for honky-tonk areas at future world's fairs and for the present-day commercial strip (Rubin 1979). However, the civic center concept was the dominant image of the City Beautiful Movement.

Cities were encouraged to develop civic spaces surrounded by public buildings — libraries, city halls and post offices, as well as museums and railroad stations — all of which were to be joined by parks, broad, tree-lined avenues, and plazas. Many cities, in fact, developed City Beautiful plans. Elected officials and business leaders viewed civic and cultural centers as an aid to business which would increase property values. Moreover, they would ". . . promote tourism, enlarge trade and generally revitalize the local economy" (Peterson 1976:430). Such projects also created opportunities for slum clearance.

City Beautiful plans were so monumental and expensive that few were realized. Cleveland, Kansas City, San Francisco, and Philadelphia had such redevelopment, while many other cities, such as Seattle and New York, never implemented their plans. In cities where civic centers were built, for example Kansas City, Missouri (Wilson 1964), some slums were cleared, and a major focal point of the city was established, a new land use which dominated the surrounding area. However, the enduring importance of the City Beautiful Movement lies not so much in the plans developed and the few projects implemented but in the image-creating potential of its ideas, exemplified by

New York City's Lincoln Center and Boston's Government Center of the 1960's.

In addition to the City Beautiful Movement, between 1890 and the early 1900's over two thousand 'improvement societies' were established to enhance the urban environment through municipal art, beautification of the outdoors through landscaping, and various civic improvements ranging from flower beds and fencing to rest rooms and electric lighting (Peterson 1976). Although minor in scale, these projects changed the visual image of many urban environments and represented a noteworthy pride in place. Civic beautification, however, was oriented toward residential neighborhoods, rather than civic centers, commercial districts, or urban parks. By the 1920's, the original City Beautiful Movement had waned. No further government efforts to redevelop the urban environment were undertaken until the 1930's.

Slum Clearance, Jobs, and Public Housing

From the turn of the century to 1929, the United States experienced economic prosperity, industrialization, and continued urban growth. But during the 1930's, a major depression put millions out of work, created massive poverty, severely curtailed urban investment, and placed many cities on the brink of bankruptcy. With the largest numbers of unemployed and poor, cities became centers of economic stagnation and social unrest. From 1930 to 1940, the urban population increased by only 0.3 percent and the number of cities over 50,000 population increased only slightly, from 191 to 199. Residential construction in 1932 dropped 84 percent from its average in the preceding decade (Keith 1973:22). Vacancy rates were high; landlords boarded up or demolished decaying buildings; thousands of properties became tax delinquent; neighborhoods deteriorated; housing was overcrowded; and squatter settlements multiplied (Friedman 1968:99). Eventually, the federal government intervened to provide jobs. Two programs in particular — public works and public housing — had major consequences.

To ameliorate unemployment and to invest in cities, Congress passed the Emergency Relief and Construction Act of 1932 to fund public works projects throughout the country. The program was eventually placed in the Works Progress Administration (WPA). A major objective was to provide work relief for the unemployed through the construction of public projects. Before its demise in the early 1940's, the WPA undertook 240,000 projects, employed more than 20 million people, and disbursed $3.068 billion (United States Federal Works Agency 1942). Projects included 62,100 buildings, 10,900 playgrounds, 45,000 miles of new and reconstructed urban roads, 4,700 parks, 17,911 miles of new storm and sanitary sewers, 970 stadiums, and 132 hospitals. More than half of the grants were spent in the fifty largest cities which then contained one-quarter of the United States population (Gelfand 1975:45).

Within cities, public works were often used to clear slums. Slums were considered a health hazard, a poor economic use of the land, and a generator of anti-social behavior. Wood (1935) estimated that 36 percent of the nation's housing stock in 1930 required replacement or substantial rehabilitation. With high vacancy rates in slums and the need for job-producing public works, slum clearance with replacement by a park, new street or playground seemed a worthwhile act. Public works, it was hoped, would also increase land values and attract investment.

Public works projects included construction of low-income housing. The 1932 Emergency Relief Act allowed the Reconstruction Finance Corporation to make loans to limited-dividend corporations to provide low-income housing and to clear slums. A single project, Knickerbocker Village, was built, consisting of 1,593 apartments on the site of what had been one of the worst slums in New York City (Friedman 1968:89). In 1932, the National Recovery Act created a Housing Division within the Public Works Administration. The Division was authorized to condemn land, clear it of slums, and build low-income housing. In Atlanta, Georgia, the first *public* slum clearance and low-rent housing project in the country was developed (United States Public Works Administration 1939:208). Under the Housing Division, more than 10,000 substandard dwelling units were demolished, and 21,700 units of low-rent housing were built, at a cost of $137 million (Friedman 1968:103).

The Housing Act passed in 1937 established the United States Housing Authority (USHA) to subsidize the construction of decent, safe, and sanitary dwellings through local public housing authorities. The legislation stipulated that public housing could not be built unless an equivalent number of unsafe or unsanitary housing units were demolished. This ". . . 'equivalent elimination' provision, in effect, removed any possibility that public housing would become a large-scale resettlement program, moving the poor into the suburban fringe. Projects would be located in slum areas where substandard housing would be cleared and vacant land used for public housing" (Friedman 1968:112). Thus the program was intended to clear slums, upgrade housing, and provide jobs (Straus 1945). By 1941, the USHA had built 73,132 dwelling units and eliminated 78,750, most of these in cities.

It was not just through the elimination of slums and the construction of new housing that the public housing program affected the urban landscape. After the passage of the 1949 Housing and Slum Clearance Act, public housing projects became large-scale, multi-storied apartment complexes, departing from the earlier small-scale, low-rise buildings (Birch 1978). The projects were often located in lower- rather than middle-class neighborhoods, in part to keep the poor, particularly Blacks, from residing in other areas of the city (Meyerson and Banfield 1955). Thus public housing projects were used to perpetuate and even intensify residential segregation. Social pathologies (crime, family disorganization) were concentrated, contributing to further deterioration of surrounding neighborhoods and of the projects themselves (Rainwater 1970). Public housing thereby became a focal image in perception of the ghetto, symbolized by poverty, crime, family disorganization, and juvenile delinquency.

Central City Decline

Economic prosperity during the decades following the Second World War notwithstanding, many central cities experienced rapid decline which generated renewed interest in urban redevelopment. From 1950 to 1970, the proportion of national population in central cities fell by 5 percent, while suburbs increased their share by 11 percent (Gorham and Glazer 1976:17). Smaller cities continued to grow, with the number exceeding 50,000 increasing from 232 to 396. The more affluent middle class was migrating to the suburbs, and rural Blacks, many of them unskilled, moved from the South to central cities in the northeast and north central states — a net increase in central city population of 362,000 between 1955 and 1970 (Gorham and Glazer 1976:16).

Interregional and intrametropolitan shifts of population greatly affected the largest central cities. As the more affluent urban population took up residence in the suburbs, commercial activity in the central cities declined. Retail sales growth in these cities between 1954 and 1967 was generally less than one-half of that which occurred in the surrounding suburbs (Committee on Banking, Housing and Urban Affairs 1973:31). This out-migration of middle class households and consumer dollars was accompanied by the exodus of industry. Unemployment was higher in central cities than in the suburbs; the gap between urban and suburban incomes increased. The movement of the rural Black and unskilled White populations into the central cities was given impetus by the increased mechanization of agriculture and the diminishing number of small farms as land holdings were consolidated. The causes of this urban decline were numerous, and debate continues concerning the relative importance of various contributing factors.[4]

One of the most important factors in suburban growth was federal insurance of residential mortgages provided by the Federal Housing Administration, created in 1934 (Gelfand 1975:216-22). The program insured residential mortgages for middle-class households that wished to purchase single family homes. During the 1930's and 1940's, the program was relatively under-utilized. The Depression and the Second World War halted investment in new housing. But after the war, the return of soldiers, increase in marriages and births, and accumulated consumer demand brought about an accelerated demand for new housing. The American Dream became a single family house on its own lot in a low density environment. Since new housing construction took place primarily in suburban areas, FHA mortgages, supplemented by Veterans Administration (VA) mortgages, thus became a major factor in post-World War II suburbanization.

Urban freeway and intercity superhighway construction was limited prior to the Fifties. The interstate highway system, initiated in 1956, provided for the construction of limited-access highways within and between major cities. Also prior to the development of this transportation network, private investment in inner city mass transit had begun to diminish. Moreover, increased affluence helped to spur the purchase and utilization of private automobiles, a means of conveyance ideally suited to low-density, suburban development. The 'pull' to the suburbs was strengthened by the construction of shopping centers at intersections of major highways and by the 'push' of an increasingly undesirable central-city environment. The suburban shopping mall attracted the consumer away from central business districts and exacerbated their decline.

Paralleling the out-migration of commerce and middle-class residents from the central cities was the suburbanization and interregional movement of industry. As the consumers became suburban, production moved closer to its markets. Skilled labor migrated to the suburbs, and so did employers. With the shift in the economy towards services and away from manufacturing, as well as a general growth which spawned new economic activities, many new firms appeared which could more easily find cheap land in ample amounts in the suburbs or in other regions. Manufacturing employment, which had focused on the northeast industrial and 'manufacturing belt' states in the Forties, shifted southward. By 1970, states such as the Carolinas and Tennessee had a similar percentage of population employed in manufacturing as Michigan or Illinois. The proportion so engaged in New York and New Jersey fell dramatically (Winsberg 1980).

---

[4]For a more thorough treatment see Ashton (1978), Castells (1976), Clawson (1975), Committee on Banking, Housing and Urban Affairs (1973:19-38), Congressional Budget Office (1978), Fusfield (1968), Sawers (1975), Sternlieb and Hughes (1975), and U. S. Department of Housing and Urban Development (1978:7-42).

Technology also played a role in the suburbanization and interregional migration of industry. With increasing mechanization, the demand for unskilled urban labor diminished. New factory technology, particularly the horizontal production line, required more ground space and thus led to a search for cheap suburban land. Furthermore, changing communications and information processing technologies made centrality less critical. For manufacturing industries whose location had been mainly influenced by proximity to raw materials, markets, or a specific labor force, improvements in road transportation helped to homogenize economic space. The locational advantages of ports and railroad centers became less crucial with the rapid growth of truck hauling and the development of innovations in containerization. With the deterioration of the rail system and the increased congestion of urban streets, movement of goods in cities became more difficult and costly. To this deficiency of the cities must be added higher property taxes, congestion, pollution, and the greater local political autonomy of suburbs which gave private enterprise greater control over development. While there is no consensus about the relative importance of these factors in suburbanization, it is incontestable that the consequences for central cities were decidedly negative.

Subsidized Redevelopment, 1949-1970

With the decline of central cities, municipal officials and business groups pressured the federal government to intervene. The response, Urban Renewal, began with the 1949 Housing Act, later modified by the Housing Act of 1954, which made federal funds available to local renewal authorities for slum clearance and urban redevelopment (Gelfand 1975:205-56; Sanders 1980). Local authorities were granted the use of eminent domain to condemn and acquire property in blighted areas, demolish existing structures, and provide new streets and utilities. Cleared land was then sold to developers at a reduced price. The federal government paid most of the difference between that price and the cost of acquiring and preparing the land (the 'write-down'). Urban redevelopment was government subsidized and promoted while its direction was left primarily in the hands of private investors. From 1949 to 1974, close to $10 billion was spent on over 2,000 urban renewal projects in approximately 1,250 cities throughout the United States (United States Department of Housing and Urban Development 1975).

Urban renewal was meant not only to enhance the economic viability of the city but also to clear slums and expand the supply of low-rent housing. Prior to 1954, accomplishments were fewer than expected. Private investors were reluctant to participate because of restrictions which oriented projects toward housing, not the most lucrative of investments, and because projects took many years to complete, tying up capital for long periods. As a result, some cities used their programs solely to clear slums. Urban Renewal thus earned the reputation of a 'bulldozer approach' to urban redevelopment — clearance without replacement (Anderson 1964).

With the Housing Act of 1954, Urban Renewal became more attractive to private investors. "Profits, not the amelioration of the pathology of the slums, were to be the goal of the revised program" (Gelfand 1975:172). Civic centers, convention halls, sports arenas, office buildings, middle and upper income housing, restaurants, department stores, and other facilities catering to the affluent became the components of projects across the country. Slums and blighted areas adjoining existing central business districts were cleared and replaced with new land uses for a new class of people.

From 1949 to 1974, 500,000 housing units were demolished and 100,000 businesses closed in the interest of these profit-making activities (Sanders 1980:119).

The consequences of urban renewal were not only economic (new jobs, more tax revenues) and physical (more new buildings, different land use patterns) but also social (Gans 1965). Because of the greater concentration of Blacks in slum housing, the elimination of slums by urban renewal became criticized for being 'Negro Removal.' Blacks, as well as poor Whites and elderly, were evicted from renewal sites and relocated in areas where rents were often higher and housing quality poor (Gans 1959; Hartman 1979). Relocation sites became overcrowded, with subsequent deterioration. Replacing the Blacks in renewal areas were White, middle-class apartment dwellers, suburban office workers, affluent shoppers and theater-goers, and out-of-town conventioneers. Thus minorities and the poor remained segregated from the middle and upper classes. City buildings reflected this situation — shiny steel and sparkling concrete structures for the middle class, deteriorated housing in blighted neighborhoods for the poor.

The criticisms of urban renewal were many. It destroyed the homes and neighborhoods of the poor and minorities; it displaced small businesses and demolished habitable housing; it directed too much investment to central business districts and not enough to positive actions in the neighborhoods; and it gave too little attention to social concerns. Numerous legislative acts after 1954 called for modifications in the program as well as new, small-scale programs which would encourage cities to plan more comprehensively for redevelopment and to give greater attention to housing rehabilitation rather than demolition. These efforts to 'soften' the negative impacts of renewal and redirect investment to the neighborhood were focused in Title I of the Demonstration Cities and Metropolitan Development Act of 1966, which created the Model Cities program (Frieden and Kaplan 1975).

Model Cities, like its many predecessors in the urban redevelopment arena, had multiple goals: the elimination of slums and blight and the provision of housing, the expansion of job opportunities, better health, improved educational and social services, reduction in crime, and general upgrading of the living conditions in marginal neighborhoods. The emphasis on physical rebuilding was supplemented by an attention to social renewal. Low income residents were to be organized in order to plan for the physical, economic, and social rehabilitation of their neighborhood. All governmental programs impinging upon that area were to be coordinated in a concerted effort to reverse the neighborhood's decline and move its residents out of poverty. Model Cities would provide funds for planning and coordination, citizen participation, and innovative progams, while other urban programs would provide housing, new sidewalks, commercial rehabilitation, and expanded social services. Before its demise in 1974, the program funded 153 neighborhoods in 151 cities and spent $2.5 billion (Committee on Banking, Housing and Urban Affairs 1973:173). By emphasizing structural rehabilitation and neighborhood preservation, it provided a viable alternative to previous central-city economic development schemes.

During the period of Urban Renewal and Model Cities, the Interstate Highway Act of 1956 funded nearly 5,000 miles of limited-access highways in urban areas, demolishing or dividing scores of neighborhoods (Gelfand 1975:222-34). With the objective of linking cities by high-speed highways which would facilitate commerce and enhance national defense, this act provided 90 percent federal construction reimbursement. Many city governments, believing that such highways would eliminate traffic congestion and make the city more accessible to suburbanites, aggressively pursued this program. The result, however, was often increased urban congestion because of large volumes of traffic moving onto narrow city streets. "Not only did the paving over of vast stretches of urban land remove valuable properties from the municipal tax rolls, but, by dumping huge numbers of cars downtown, the expressways produced an insatiable thirst for more parking space that disfigured the central business districts" (Gelfand 1975:228). Urban highways also made it easier for suburbanites to commute to work in the city. Moreover, drivers could now traverse suburbia more quickly, facilitating the rise of the suburban shopping mall. Malls captured consumer purchases from the central city and contributed to the decline of urban commercial districts.

Highway construction destroyed urban neighborhoods by demolishing housing and placing physical barriers between residents of the same neighborhood (Lupo *et al.* 1971). To minimize project cost, highway planners searched for inexpensive land with the least costly buildings where little organized resistance could be expected. Lower- and working-class neighborhoods with marginal or dilapidated buildings met these criteria. Between 1965 and 1976, federally-aided highway construction demolished 104,148 dwellings and displaced 305,334 persons, the great majority in urban areas (Altshuler 1979:341). From 1967 to 1970, nearly 12,000 businesses were displaced (Leavitt 1970:265).

Severe social damage resulted from urban freeway construction. Those uprooted from their neighborhoods frequently moved to less desirable environments. Neighborhood social patterns were disrupted, local employment reduced, and local commercial facilities and organizations eliminated. Left in their place were multilane highways, often large concrete structures with few pedestrian crossings. In cities throughout the United States — Dayton, Wilmington, Providence, San Francisco — one can easily see the esthetic damage and surmise the social, economic, and physical destruction which took place.

Urban Renewal and expressways were expected to reverse the declining fortunes of central cities; however, both contributed to burgeoning social and economic problems. Cities were not transformed into foci of economic growth. Model Cities, moreover, was not able to stabilize inner-city neighborhoods. Instead, urban conditions worsened with interregional shifts of population, employment, and investment, and a weakened fiscal condition.

Interregional Shifts and Fiscal Crisis

The 1970's was a decade of economic stagnation. The country experienced recessions in 1975 and 1980. High unemployment and double-digit inflation eroded the financial positions of households and businesses. The rate of national population growth declined, and the proportion of elderly people increased. The cities were also struggling. Although out-migration slowed, from 1970 to 1977 central city population decreased by 4.6 percent while suburban population increased by 12.0 percent (Sternlieb and Hughes 1979a:627). Regional population and investment shifts further weakened the social and economic condition of many cities, particularly in the Northeast and North Central states (Figure 1).

The decline of the Northeast and North Central 'Industrial Crescent' and the rise of the West and South has been underway for at least fifty years.[5] These regional shifts

---

[5]For an analysis of the causes of interregional shifts see Fainstein and Fainstein (1976), Melman (1977), Sale (1977), Sternleib and Hughes (1978), and Sternlieb and Hughes (1975).

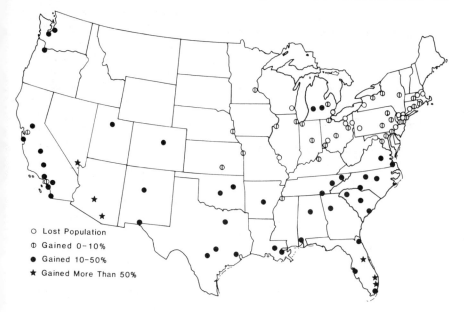

FIGURE 1   POPULATION CHANGE IN THE 100 LARGEST
STANDARD METROPOLITAN STATISTICAL AREAS, 1970-1980
(U. S. Census Information Service)

may have begun with the quest for western and southern climatic amenities, but a central condition has been the regional movement of industry. Many businesses have migrated out of the Industrial Crescent to take advantage of the lower rate of unionization in the southern and western states, a lower cost of living which allows for lower wages, and a perceived 'business climate' more conducive to private enterprise. Energy is cheaper and supplies more reliable in these states since many have ample natural gas and oil and less severe winters. Companies have begun to take federal environmental regulations into consideration when locating their plants. Meeting stringent environmental standards is, in general, more costly in the already degraded and developed northern industrial areas.

The Sunbelt has also been the recipient of high technology industries and of governmental assistance. The aero-space industry has been concentrated in this region, given a major impetus by the growth in California of the airplane industry during World War II and the establishment of the space center in Houston in the Sixties. Electronics is an important growth industry in the South and Southeast, while the Midwest and South have benefitted from agribusiness growth. Governmental expenditures for space and military contracts and military bases in the western and southern states and funding of major water projects in these regions spurred employment and encouraged population in-migration. Lacking strong Congressional representation on key committees, the Northeastern and North Central states have suffered. All of these factors have resulted in population shifts from the Snowbelt to the Sunbelt, more rapid employment growth in the Sunbelt, and reversal of the long-standing South-to-North Black migration.

Fiscal crisis further undermined the viability of Northeastern and North Central cities during the 1970's. Cities such as New York and Cleveland faced declining revenues, increasing expenditures, lower bond ratings, and an inability to use municipal bonds to fund social programs and physical improvements. The problem, simply stated, was one of a mismatch between revenues and expenditures leading to an inability of city governments to meet current bills (Alcaly and Bodian 1977; Schultz *et al.* 1977; Tabb 1978). Tax bases declined with the out-migration of people and firms; sales taxes yielded diminishing revenues; and there was little new investment. Added to these factors was heightened reliance on federal revenues, a dependence which increased just as the industrial cities were losing political influence in state and national legislatures.

On the other side of the fiscal equation were rising expenditures. Governments found it difficult to shrink services as population declined. Moreover, the influx of unskilled minorities and the growing elderly population meant an increased demand for services. Simultaneously, inflation made everything costlier. Municipal unions fought to keep wages in line with rising living costs. Balanced urban budgets were increasingly difficult to achieve.

Regardless of population size, distressed cities are typically Snowbelt manufacturing centers whose residential and commercial construction is relatively old. They have few large tracts of vacant land, a substantial minority population, and are surrounded by incorporated municipalities which prevent growth by annexation (U.S. Department of Housing and Urban Development 1978:40). Governmental policies in the Seventies, then, had to respond not only to urban distress but also to the regional dimension of decline.

Urban and Community Development

Urban revitalization emerged as a definable strategy for urban redevelopment during the 1970's. Two programs linked this strategy to government, Community Development Block Grants (CDBG) and Urban Development Action Grants (UDAG). CDBG grew out of President Nixon's New Federalism, an attempt to eliminate the multitude of overlapping governmental programs and to give local governments more discretion in the expenditure of federal funds. UDAG was a later response to the dispersal of federal funding generated by CDBG. A more targeted program was needed to direct monies to the most distressed cities. Both programs were oriented to place characteristics, rather than to groups of people (low income populations or minorities), and thus had intrinsic spatial consequences.

In 1974, the Housing and Community Development Act (HDCA) rearranged six urban programs into one 'block' grant (Rosenfeld 1980). Urban Renewal, Model Cities and programs involving open space, neighborhood and public facilities, and water and sewer services were collapsed into a single CDBG program. Funding for community development activities was based on entitlement rather than competition. All eligible communities would receive federal funds based on community characteristics. Although the Act specified broad national goals, local communities were given considerable discretion over expenditures.

During fiscal year 1979, 3,305 grants representing close to $4 billion were awarded to three thousand communities and urban counties (Nenno 1980). Of the total expenditures, 42 percent went for public works and 30 percent was allocated for private property rehabilitation. In terms of program objectives, the largest amount of funding was devoted to the elimination of slums and blight, the second largest to the conservation of the housing stock. CDBG also includes economic development, social services, housing construction, and historic preservation.

From a spatial perspective, CDBG has some interesting implications. First, the entitlement procedures create an overall distribution of funding highly responsive to more distressed communities (Bunce 1980). Second, the program requires that at least 50 percent of funds be spent to benefit low- and moderate-income people. However, a number of local governments have managed to undertake projects, such as bridle paths in county parks, which do not. Third, as an attempt to deal with such practices, the federal government in 1978 allowed localities to concentrate expenditures in low and moderate income neighborhoods through the Neighborhood Strategies Area (NSA) program. This program allows the community to obtain more funds, and also to target CDBG expenditures. Finally, by emphasizing neighborhood preservation and housing rehabilitation rather than slum clearance, CDBG has caused less displacement and disruption of neighborhoods than, for example, Urban Renewal.

The UDAG program more closely resembles Urban Renewal. Passed as a 1977 amendment to the HCDA, it provides capital grants to communities primarily for economic development through expansion of the employment and tax bases (Gist 1980). Funds go mainly to distressed cities and urban counties for investment in public and private facilities. An essential component of the application for a UDAG is a commitment from a private investor to participate in the project. By early 1980, 692 grants had been authorized totalling $1.3 billion (American Industrial Priorities Report 1980). This money is estimated to have leveraged $7.4 billion in private funds, created 206,652 new and permanent jobs, retained 92,025 jobs, generated 161,660 construction jobs, and provided 50,000 units of housing.[6] The industrial, commercial, and neighborhood projects funded were spread across 398 cities. Early projects were mostly hotels built to attract conventions and tourists. Displacement occurred in many cases, and slum clearance frequently accompanied new office and commercial structures in central cities.

In its emphasis on targeting distressed cities, UDAG has explicitly spatial goals. Holcomb and Beauregard (1980a; 1980b) show, however, that the strength of the targeting was diluted by political considerations during the passage and funding of the enabling legislation and by the requirement that private investment be leveraged. To obtain support from non-urbanized states, for example, the legislation reserved twenty-five percent of UDAG funds for cities of under 50,000 people. Moreover, distress criteria which cities must meet to be eligible for UDAG funds are not very discriminating — 80 percent of metropolitan cities can qualify. Applications are screened for 'feasibility and effectiveness' (for example, the size and strength of private sector commitment) before more stringent distress measures are used as selection criteria. In addition, an amendment passed in 1980 qualifies some of the previously ineligible cities to apply for funding if they contain 'pockets of poverty.' This further dilutes the targeting to the most distressed cities.

---

[6]The term 'leveraging' refers to the enticement of private dollars into the development process by the investment of public dollars. Of utmost concern is the leveraging ratio, the ratio between private and public dollars. The higher the ratio, the more successful the program. Leveraging was not a requirement of earlier redevelopment projects.

Closely following CDBG and UDAG was the development of new national policy on cities and on neighborhoods. In March 1978, President Carter released his National Urban Policy (U.S. Department of Housing and Urban Development 1978). It reaffirmed the nation's commitment to urban development; called for partnership of government, private investors, neighborhood groups, and voluntary associations to further urban development; and presented a series of policy proposals. The actual consequences of this policy, however, were miniscule. Lacking a constituency, the major programmatic recommendations languished in Congress. The report of the National Commission on Neighborhoods (1979) had the same fate. It called for reinvestment in neighborhoods, economic development, more human services, development of mechanisms for neighborhood governance, and an end to racial discrimination. The political climate surrounding its release was not conducive for any concerted action; no major legislation emerged.

The Seventies thus ended on a note of hope based upon federal recognition of the needs of cities and neighborhoods and on numerous revitalization efforts throughout the country, but accompanied by chords of despair because of inaction on national policy and the continued city decline. For example, in 1980 another commission established by President Carter reported its findings (President's Commission for a National Agenda for the Eighties 1980). Its members called for the federal government to support migration from declining cities and regions to growing ones. This was bad news for Snowbelt cities. However, the report quickly became obsolete as President Reagan proposed fewer domestic programs and a diminished involvement of the federal government in urban affairs. Additionally, he proposed stimulating the private sector to increase investment. As the country continued in a recessionary trough during the early Eighties, it became increasingly difficult to replace despair with hope.

The history of urban decline and redevelopment in the United States points out a strong relationship among these processes, private sector investments, and governmental actions. Redevelopment seldom occurs without the simultaneous support of government and private investors. Neither can nor is willing to act alone. Moreover, each phase of urban decline sets new conditions for another round of redevelopment activity. These facets of urban redevelopment will become even more striking as we explore urban revitalization more fully.

3

Extent and Causes of Revitalization

'Urban revitalization' labels a diverse set of processes currently taking place in American cities. Built upon the legacy of preceding redevelopment efforts, revitalization incorporates many of their successes, certain new initiatives, and even some of their less dismal failures. Compared to the Urban Renewal program, urban revitalization has more varied components, relies more on market behavior (particularly in decisions about neighborhood rehabilitation), and depends less upon governmental initiative. Urban revitalization is not confined, as were many Urban Renewal plans, to a single, large project. It often comprises private sector redevelopment of the central business district, neighborhood commercial redevelopment, and smaller scale, private and governmental neighborhood renovations. Revitalization is a complex phenomenon which is seldom articulated into an integrated redevelopment effort. How extensive is revitalization, and what processes explain its occurrence?

Scale and Location of Revitalization

Urban revitalization efforts have many underlying similarities, but there are also significant differences from city to city in response to unique economic, political, social, and historical realities (Beauregard and Holcomb 1979). As a result, devising a common measure for comparison is extremely difficult. Some quantitative indicators have been used as surrogates for revitalization, for example, the in-migration of affluent population groups, changes in the amount of professional employment within the city, rehabilitation of the housing stock, rising housing values, and increased tax revenues from property sales. Qualitative and anecdotal data, consisting of reports on the multitude of revitalization activities such as central business district projects, gentrifying neighborhoods, and new public works, have been used. Thus, the scale and location of urban revitalization throughout the United States can be outlined, but it can not be thoroughly described in a quantitative way.

The limited statistical evidence for urban revitalization in cities of the United States is ambiguous at best. Several authors have pointed out that the number of households in central cities has increased, often at apparently healthy rates (Abravanel and Mancini 1980; Fossett and Nathan 1980; Sternlieb and Hughes 1979a, 1979b). Because the average size of households is smaller, this increase does not offset overall urban population decline. If new households are composed largely of young professionals with few children — the stereotypical 'back to the city' migrant — then an increase in disposable income, rents, and tax revenues would bode well for the economic recovery of central cities. It appears, however, that these upwardly mobile, gentrifying professionals constitute only a small portion of new urban households. Instead, most migrants to central cities continue to be from lower-income, minority groups, while out-migrants have somewhat higher income and are racially mixed (Spain 1980). Because of declining population and the differential incomes between in- and out-migrants, central cities experienced a net loss of $26.9 billion in aggregate personal income between 1970 and 1974 (Sternlieb and Hughes 1979b:4). Further hindering a widespread revitalization of cities was a decline in central city employment between 1970 and 1977 while suburban and rural employment was increasing.

Despite aggregate statistics that reveal little sign of central city revival, various studies have indicated that localized urban areas are experiencing intensive renovation. A study of the downtown areas of the twenty largest cities in the United States found evidence of a resurgence of middle- and upper-status neighborhoods, especially in cities without heavy industry and with administrative central business districts and significant commuting distances from the suburbs (Lipton 1980). A mail and telephone survey conducted in 1979 by the Urban Land Institute found that 86 percent of cities over 150,000 population had housing renovation activities (Black 1980). In addition, during the Seventies, housing values, home ownership, and home maintenance activity, all indices of housing demand, were growing in central cities relative to the suburbs (James 1980). Professional journals and the popular media frequently report gentrifying neighborhoods to which young professionals with few children are moving. While some migrate from the suburbs to inner-city neighborhoods, for the most part these are intracity moves as renters resettle as homeowners in renovating neighborhoods (Black 1980; Brozen 1979; Clay 1980; Gale 1980).

Many cities have commercial and industrial redevelopment projects, as well as public works. Certain commercial projects are widely known — Boston's Faneuil Hall and San Francisco's Ghirardelli Square. Others are in smaller and less publicized locations — the corporate headquarters and hotel-convention center in New Brunswick, New Jersey; the restoration of the opera hall and historic railroad station in Van Buren, Arkansas. Increasingly we hear reports of old factories being renovated and new plants constructed. General Motors is building a $500 million Cadillac plant in Detroit on the site of a former Chrysler factory (Sherrin 1980). Minneapolis has received an Urban Development Action Grant to expand an engraving plant which employs several hundred local residents; a major industrial park is being developed in the South Bronx. Some cities are including public works projects in their revitalization schemes. San Diego is constructing a trolley system; Seminole, Oklahoma, is installing new street lighting and sidewalks in the downtown area.

A comprehensive inventory of such commercial and industrial projects and public works is lacking. The distribution of UDAG funds is a useful surrogate measure. A few major redevelopment schemes were financed entirely by private sources (Renaissance Center in Detroit). Most projects have at least some public subsidy, and UDAG has been the program most directed to the redevelopment of distressed cities (Holcomb and Beauregard 1980a). UDAG funds are concentrated in the Northeastern and North Central states, and in central cities rather than in suburbs or communities outside metropolitan areas (Jacobs and Roistacher 1980). However, central cities in most metropolitan areas have received grants, thus indicating that revitalization is geographically widespread.

FIGURE 2 DISTRIBUTION OF PUBLICIZED REVITALIZATION ACTIVITIES (Beauregard and Cousins 1981, using *HUD Challenge, Journal of Housing,* and *Planning* for the years 1970-1980)

A qualitative indicator of revitalization efforts is their presentation in professional journals (Beauregard and Cousins 1981). Figure 2 is a cartographic compilation of revitalization activities reported in three urban journals for the years 1970 through 1980. Most of the publicized revitalization activity is concentrated in the Northeastern and North Central states, with a secondary cluster in California. Of 108 cities mentioned, almost forty percent are in the Northeast. Publicized revitalization appears to be more characteristic of larger than of smaller cities. Slightly more than fifty percent of cities mentioned had populations over 100,000 in 1975, and only fifteen percent had fewer than 25,000 people.

The pattern which emerges is small islands of revitalization appearing within otherwise declining central cities. Revitalization on some scale seems to be geographically widespread, with large cities and those in the northeast experiencing a greater incidence of revitalization than others (Black 1980; Grier and Grier 1980:260). The most optimistic interpretation is that urban revitalization, presently limited in scale, is the beginning of an enduring trend in urban recovery. More pessimistically, it could represent a minor perturbation in the downward spiral of urban decline. "Even in the most improved cities, the same old problems remain — from budget deficits and deteriorating water mains to troubled schools and a larger welfare class" (Alpern 1979:28). Moreover, Fossett and Nathan (1980) measured continued urban distress in terms of unemployment, educational level, income, housing density, poverty, and population composition, even in those cities with highly touted revitalization efforts.

Conventional Explanations

Explanations for revitalization are not well developed. For the most part, theorists and policymakers have been content to explain the 'return to the city' or, at least, decreasing out-migration. Explanations for why developers and investors have redis-covered the city as a locus for investment are rudimentary. Moreover, no consensus exists as to the significance of various factors contributing to revitalization, and, thus, many partial explanations are offered (U.S. Department of Housing and Urban Development 1978:44-59).

For middle-class households, there are both 'pull' factors which increase the relative locational advantages of central cities and 'push' factors making suburban and non-metropolitan residence less attractive. The burgeoning cost of energy has made commuting and the maintenance of a single family suburban home increasingly expen-sive. The energy crisis coincided with demographic and economic changes which invigorated the demand for the smaller housing units more typical of the urban housing stock. While overall population growth has slowed in the central cities, new household formation has expanded rapidly as the 'baby boom' generation has matured. Thus the number of households in central cities rose by 6.3 percent while household size decreased from 3.47 to 3.30 persons in the sevenyear period between 1970 and 1977 (Sternlieb and Hughes 1979b).

The more affluent new urban households have abandoned the quest for an expensive surburban home. Instead they search out old, relatively inexpensive, but sound, housing in inner-city neighborhoods. They then undertake its rehabilitation and the area's overall gentrification. Many affluent professionals are not concerned simply with these economic issues but also with the opportunities for an urbane life-style which a city, particularly a revitalized city, offers. Moreover, a combination of recessions slowing new housing construction, inflation and high mortgage interest rates making newly-built housing extremely expensive, and increased housing demand, with rapid household formation rates, has acted to direct households and developers to older urban neighborhoods. Meanwhile, a general surge in the price of housing in the Seventies made purchase an attractive investment, a defensive strategy in a period of high inflation.

Within the urban population, several groups are becoming increasingly important for new housing demand and for revitalization activities. One such group is young, childless professionals, living alone or with a partner, attracted to city amenities, who may move into rehabilitated housing in gentrifying areas either as renters or owners. The increasing rate of female labor force participation and the delay in childbearing age makes an urban residence more attractive (Holcomb 1981). A central location minimizes commuting costs for two-employee households. With fewer children, private schools become financially feasible, decreasing the importance of public school qual-ity. Elderly and female-headed households are also growing components of the urban population, the latter increasing by 27.5 percent between 1970 and 1977. While these households are not often viewed as desirable in revitalization efforts (they tend to have weak labor force participation and relatively low incomes), they do contribute to housing demand, and indirectly bring about rehabilitation and new development.

Changes in the economy and governmental policies also stimulated commercial and industrial reinvestment in cities. With a high rate of inflation accompanied by slow economic growth, benefits of conserving existing central city investments became increasingly apparent. The presence of an elaborate infrastructure, moreover, increases the comparative advantage of cities over undeveloped outer suburbs, and the differential between urban and suburban land prices is narrowing. Tax incentives for plant expansion and renovation encourage investment in both cities and suburbs, but increasingly urban governments are packaging various financial incentives and other assistance (job training) to retain businesses in the city. In the late Seventies the dollar decline relative to other currencies made the U.S. attractive to both domestic and foreign investors (U. S. Department of Housing and Urban Development 1979a). By the early Eighties, the dollar's value increased, but high interest rates continued to attract foreign investment. A number of major Canadian investors and developers have moved into the United States in search of profitable investment opportunities. Cadillac-Fairview has proposed a $1 billion redevelopment in Los Angeles; Olympia-York has purchased office buildings in Manhattan; and numerous Canadian investors are involved in the surge of construction in downtown Denver.

Changes in employment structure have increased the proportion of people engaged in professional, administrative, and service occupations and reduced that in manufacturing. Much of this employment is located in cities. Thus, some cities are generating new employment faster than, or at least as fast as, many suburban areas (Abravanel and Mancini 1980:30). Urban employment, coupled with commuting costs, may further encourage people to reside within central cities. Most states in the Northeast still send more tax dollars to Washington than are returned, but the preceding decade witnessed an expansion in the number of economic development and social programs directed at assisting distressed cities. By 1978, federal aid as a proportion of local revenues was forty percent or higher in many urban communities (U. S. Department of Housing and Urban Development 1978:101). Some programs, such as UDAG, were targeted to cities precisely for the purpose of stimulating revitalization.

At the same time, various 'push' factors have reduced the attraction of suburbia for new investment. Inflation in the construction industry and rising mortgage rates have put the purchase of new surburban homes beyond the financial reach of most households. Suburban communities are increasingly resisting new development because of adverse environmental and social impacts. Land use regulations to protect agricultural land and watersheds, and exclusionary zoning which keep out lower income households are characteristic strategies. Land and development become more costly, making urban locations more attractive. Many inner-ring suburbs are beginning to experience urban ills. Increasing crime rates, higher taxes, and pollution have invaded these communities and further diminished their relative advantages (Allman 1978). Outer-ring suburbs and non-metropolitan areas continue to offer many amenities and to attract new residents, although the absolute numbers are not large.

The factors cited are usually advanced in explanation of urban revitalization and the return to the city. For various reasons, home buyers and renters, property developers, investors, store owners, industrialists, and governmental officials are making decisions which may expand urban investment and rejuvenate parts of cities, economically and socially. There is, however, another perspective.

An Alternative Perspective

The preceding explanations of urban revitalization conform to conventional urban analysis in the United States. This mode of analysis, based in mainstream urban sociology and urban geography, has come under attack in the last few years (Castells

1975; Peet 1977b; Slater 1977). The treatment of two issues will convey the nature of an alternative, and still rudimentary, perspective: first, the general presence of revitalization efforts in cities and, second, those factors which explain the redevelopment of urban neighborhoods.

Cities can be viewed as the physical manifestation of the requirements and consequences of how the production of goods and services is organized within society. That is, to understand urban form and its changes, one must look initially at the structure and functioning of the economy, and then consider social relations, political activities, cultural dispositions, and consumer preferences. Of course, the relative importance of each of these factors in explaining urban development and redevelopment varies historically and by city. Regardless, a common theme is the importance of economic relations in determining urban form. Thus space under capitalism, as one particular form of economic organization, might be seen as organized by its requirements for production and distribution, by the class conflicts based in the workplace and manifested in consumption issues (housing protests), and by the intervention of the government to preserve the economy and to control social unrest and political conflict (Soja 1980). By the organization of space is meant not only the use of land but also the types of investment made in various buildings and structures such as highways and bridges.

To David Harvey (1973:238), for example, cities are the ". . . built forms created out of the mobilization, extraction and geographic concentration of significant quantities of the socially designated surplus product." The surplus product is those material resources beyond requirements for basic subsistence. Cities emerge from the need for capitalism to concentrate spatially the circulation of wealth, commodities, and information in order to reduce the friction of distance and, thus, speed the return of capital to productive activities after it has been used for other types of expenditure (Lamarche 1976). Cities will vary in structure and functions under different modes of economic organization (Harvey 1973:245-74) and within stages of capitalism itself (Gordon 1978). Simply stated, the city is a device for enhancing the accumulation of wealth. It is also an arena of competition for the acquisition and control of space. Since urban land use is also partially determined by economic relations, any analysis of urban form and change must be based on an understanding of how production of goods and services is organized.

Using this theoretical perspective, revitalization activities are interpreted as facilitating capital accumulation, representing the struggle of various classes for space and for access to public services and private amenities, and revealing the role of the government in balancing the interests of capital against those of labor. Mollenkopf (1978) argues that redevelopment efforts constitute attempts to resolve a dual crisis of declining central-city land values and a shortfall in governmental revenues. New public and private investment is spawned by pro-growth coalitions of business elites and politicians to increase the value of central-city land and to revive the tax base. By engaging in urban redevelopment, the uneasy social peace and political cohesion within the city is threatened. Displacement, channeling of government funds to large-scale developers, and neglect of residential neighborhoods create discontent. Urban redevelopment thus brings about new crises.

Harvey (1975) outlined the basic elements of the alternative, Marxist perspective on urban redevelopment. His argument was based on the role of financial institutions in facilitating the circulation of capital and on the constant search for new investment opportunities. He first posited that major investors engendered a debt structure whose payment requires that property retain its value. To this extent, high-value land in the central cities — whose development created a large debt for both developers and the public — must be redeveloped periodically in order to increase its market value and, thus, make it possible for the debt created by the initial investment to be repaid. More accurately, financial institutions face a choice between disinvesting and using capital for other investments and preserving the value of debts through reinvestment.[7] Past indebtedness thus dictates present investments. In terms of central-city land, the choice is redevelopment. The land is very valuable; the public infrastructure is too costly to reproduce elsewhere; and the property is capable of yielding high profits.

Additionally, Harvey (1977) pointed out that the capitalist social structure is not without its contradictions: Spatial structures of an earlier period may become barriers to present capital accumulation. Due to past actions of private investors and local government, the built environment of a particular location may be less profitable than another use. A factory, the highest use for land at an earlier time, might now be demolished to make way for a more appropriate office building. "Temporal crises in fixed capital investment . . . are therefore usually expressed as periodic reshapings of the geographic environment to adapt it to the needs of further accumulation" (Harvey 1977:273). Through urban redevelopment, capitalists eliminate barriers to accumulation of wealth and capture the increase in locational values brought about by historical changes in the city (Roweis and Scott 1978:57-8).

These explanations, however, focus primarily on downtown investment and do not consider the rehabilitation of neighborhoods. Neil Smith (1979) has argued that gentrification occurs in urban neighborhoods when disinvestment within that neighborhood has led to a situation in which the ground rent which could be realized through housing reinvestment exceeds the ground rent which is currently being realized. That is, potential value of the land is not being captured under the current land use. Thus, Smith casts gentrification into an economic argument recognizing the ways in which financial investments change the desirability of different locations. Residential differentiation, moreover, is maintained by what Harvey (1975) labels class-monopoly rent. Differences in rent from one area of a city to another are maintained through class power and supported by institutional structures such as banks and savings and loan associations. Economic relations are thus further reinforced by political relations.

A more specific explanation of gentrification, one which would not necessarily negate the above, focuses on the search for safe and rapidly growing housing investments on the part of an upwardly mobile middle class with employment ties to the city. Inflation of housing costs, making new housing affordable only by the rich, and high returns realized through home ownership create the conditions for gentrification. Uneven distribution of newly discovered urban amenities, such as older housing and quaint streets, then determines which neighborhoods will be gentrified. Existing lower and working class residents lack the political and economic power to resist and, as a result, are displaced.

In neighborhoods which are being upgraded and stabilized without displacement, governmental assistance programs represent actions to stem social discontent and to maintain legitimacy. These programs compenstate for governmental investment in other parts of the city and governmental assistance to private developers. The government is helping to solidify the hold on that neighborhood by the current, usually lower,

---

[7]Disinvestment refers both to the withdrawal of capital from a place, as when a company relocates its plant outside of the city, and to the lack of investment in the maintenance of buildings and equipment.

working-class, residents. This will maintain the neighborhood's position in the city's structure of residential differentiation and keep it from being 'invaded' by lower-income residents. The argument we have presented is derived from a Marxist analysis. Although Marxist urban theorists have not focused specifically on urban revitalization, their theoretical position provides a basis for explaining its occurrence. Moreover, Marxist analysis recognizes explicitly the social-justice perspective which underlies this work. It begins with the basic forces which motivate investment decisions and analyzes how these affect the distribution of economic and political power. Before exploring this alternative to conventional analysis further, we need to consider urban revitalization in greater depth.

4

Commercial Redevelopment

At the spatial, economic, and political heart of revitalizing cities is the central business district (CBD). Prior to decline, the commercial core served both the city itself and the surrounding hinterland of suburbs and small towns. People visited the CBD to work, shop, attend cultural events, and find entertainment. With out-migration of people and industry from the central city came the flight of commercial enterprises and administrative functions. Simultaneously, neighborhood commercial centers also experienced disinvestment and general deterioration. The hierarchy of marketplaces which had characterized the metropolitan area just before and immediately after World War II was transformed. Suburban shopping malls became new commercial foci. Central cities no longer offered the range of amenities which had previously made them magnets for economic and social activity.

Thus, redevelopment of central business districts and, to a lesser extent, neighborhood commercial areas, are viewed as pivotal in urban revitalization efforts. CBD redevelopment enables the central city to reassert its dominance in the economic and cultural life of the region. Neighborhood commercial revitalization adds localized services, thus further enticing the middle class to remain within, or move back to, the city. Despite the importance of both types of commercial redevelopment, CBD redevelopment receives the attention of the media, the bulk of the new investment, and the hopes of supporters of revitalization (Levy and McGrath 1979). Without a doubt, it is the central business district which economically and symbolically defines the viability of the city.

Redevelopment of retail and administrative functions, rather than manufacturing, is part of the larger strategy of urban economic development (Groton 1979; Redstone 1976; Sutton 1980). The emphasis on the service sector of the economy, rather than on goods production, mirrors changes in the national economy. In the United States, those employed in producing goods declined from 47 percent to 33 percent of the workforce from 1929 to 1977, while those delivering services increased from 55 to 68 percent. The value of services is now about equal to that of manufactured goods (Ginzberg and Vojta 1981). Although the directors of industrial firms participate in and may lead revitalization efforts (as occurred in Detroit, Toledo, Pittsburgh, and Hartford), new factories are uncommon as components of redevelopment. New administrative buildings for manufacturing firms, on the other hand, are commonly included in revitalization efforts. Proponents of revitalization recognize the transition of cities from manufacturing to service centers and focus their energies on enhancing commercial, cultural, recreational and other 'tertiary' activities (Ley, 1980, 1981; Policinski 1978).

The relatively small role of manufacturing in urban economic revitalization can be tied to several factors. The urban land market is not suited to the large blocks of relatively cheap land required for industrial plants. Manufacturing activities do not provide the professional, administrative, and high technology jobs which attract the middle class. Moreover, such firms pose environmental dilemmas and contribute little to the image of the city which proponents of revitalization wish to convey. Nevertheless, there are some exceptions, such as the industrial redevelopment in Jersey City and Yonkers, the new Cadillac Plant in Detroit, and industrial district revitalization in Philadelphia. Such industrial redevelopment projects are usually administratively and spatially separate from commercial redevelopment.

The extent of commercial redevelopment across the United States is difficult to ascertain. Innumerable magazine and newspaper articles, professional reports and research documents explore individual instances of such revitalization. No systematic assessment of the regional, urban, and temporal distribution of central business district and neighborhood commercial revitalization has been undertaken.

A preliminary assessment of commercial reinvestment resulting from the Urban Renewal program found major variations across cities and regions (Sanders 1980). Urban Renewal in some cities was primarily commercial; in others, residential redevelopment was emphasized. No distinct patterns emerged. However, this is only one governmental program, and it no longer dominates redevelopment activity. Any exploration of contemporary commercial redevelopment must recognize that funding now comes from a variety of sources ranging from Small Business Administration (SBA) loans for neighborhood stores to UDAGs for hotels. Through the first quarter of fiscal year 1979, approximately thirty-seven percent of all UDAG projects were classified as commercial. These represented about forty-five percent of all funds, of which one-eighth went to small cities. Approximately sixty to seventy metropolitan cities, then, had commercial redevelopment projects supported by UDAG as of that date. Another approximately sixty metropolitan cities had 'neighborhood' UDAGs (Gist 1980: 246). No analysis of spatial patterns exists, although one might assume that almost all revitalizing cities have commercial redevelopment underway.

Central Business District Redevelopment

Faced with competition from suburban shopping malls and the out-migration of middle-class residents and shoppers, the central business districts of declining cities suffer from numerous problems. Retail sales have diminished as fewer shoppers visit the downtown. Store owners, as a result, have disinvested or left. Blight and vacant storefronts followed. With the shrinkage of commercial activity and the deterioration of the environment, offices and service enterprises began to close or leave the city, taking with them jobs and ratables, real properties subject to local taxes. Theaters and cultural facilities could no longer draw patrons. Crime increased and the city came to be perceived as a dangerous place. No longer was the CBD the commercial, economic, cultural, and entertainment hub of the metropolis.

The solution proposed is fairly similar from one revitalizing city to the next: create an exciting, active, and vibrant central business district which will provide jobs, services, goods, and recreation through both the day and night (Redstone 1976:19). A bold statement must be made; it should take physical form. New commercial space is needed to attract shoppers. Office space will accommodate jobs for the middle-class, and luxury apartment buildings will house them. Convention centers, restaurants,

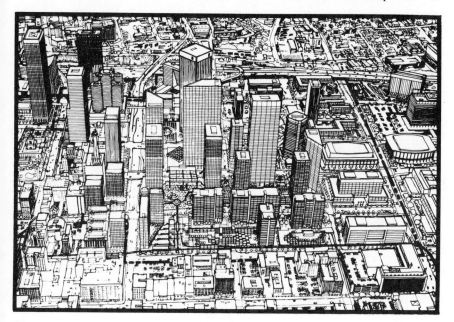

FIGURE 3 PLAN FOR THE REDEVELOPMENT OF BUNKER
HILL, LOS ANGELES (diagram by Alvin D. Jenkins, courtesy of the
Community Redevelopment Agency of the City of Los Angeles)

sports arenas, museums, and concert halls will attract recreational spending. Waterfront developments, plazas, and pedestrian malls will make visiting pleasant and
enticing, and parking garages and new freeways will make the CBD accessible. All of
these activities will generate employment for residents of the city. The benefits, it is
surmised, will accrue to the city as a whole.

The general strategy parallels the earlier Urban Renewal program, but with some
significant differences. Commercial revitalization pivots upon the formation of a
private-public partnership which brings major developers, financial institutions, and
community leaders together with elected officials and agencies of the city government
(Beauregard and Holcomb 1979). The initiative has shifted away from the Urban
Renewal agency to local community and business leaders. In Los Angeles, Pittsburgh,
Harrisburg, Detroit, Hartford, and St. Paul, public-private or solely private development
corporations have been formed to plan and implement CBD redevelopment. Multi-
block projects coalesce a variety of activities and re-define the center of the city (Figure
3).

Although government is subordinate to private initiatives, it now has at its disposal
a wider range of programs and resources for attracting private sector investment.
These include outright grants such as those from the UDAG and CDBG programs; the
use of municipal, state, and federal monies to build new roads, parking garages, sewer,
and water systems; and numerous low interest loan funds to finance private-sector
redevelopment. Government can also use eminent domain powers to accumulate large

parcels of land and may even pay land preparation costs before sale. Sometimes government actually builds and retains ownership, leasing a facility to a private firm as in the case of Baltimore's Convention Center. By making commitments to occupy part of new or renovated office buildings, government can stimulate private investment in such buildings (Milan 1976).

Tax regulations also encourage a flow of investment to CBD redevelopment. In many states, tax abatements granted to new downtown developments are intended to lure investment into declining cities. However, so many jurisdictions now offer abatements that the intended comparative locational advantage may disappear. Cities are left subsidizing private sector firms through lower property taxes (Goodman 1979). Other tax regulations which encourage redevelopment are tax increment financing and accelerated depreciation schedules which reward firms that construct new buildings.

Several states use tax increment financing, most notably California. The city government determines the project area to be restored or redeveloped, then freezes that area's tax base until completion of the redevelopment. As improvements occur, taxes on additional property value are paid by property owners but placed in a special fund to be used by the local redevelopment agency for further reinvestment in the designated area (Seline 1976:49). Tax revenues generated by the increasing value of redeveloped properties will be spent in the immediate area, an incentive for investors. Tax increment financing also poses an interesting geographical question of social justice. It also means that additional tax revenues cannot be used in other deteriorated neighborhoods of the city. Thus tax benefits from redevelopment are neither spatially nor socially redistributed.

Components of CBD Redevelopment

Commercial redevelopment efforts vary widely both in scale and content (Redstone 1976; Zambo 1975). Smaller cities may have a pedestrian mall or office complex. In larger cities redevelopment projects may cover many blocks; include a range of building types and economic, social, and cultural activities; and occur simultaneously in different parts of the city (Derthick 1972; Hartman 1974; Stone 1976).

The most common component of revitalization is the shopping facility. A commercial focus will attract shoppers into the CBD and, thus, allow the city to compete with outlying suburban shopping malls. As one commercial developer stated, downtown retailing is the ". . . essential glue of the city, the fuel that will truly fire the renaissance" (DeVito 1980:198). The earliest examples took the form of outdoor, pedestrian malls in which landscaped streets were closed to traffic and design themes were used to create harmony among storefronts. Kalamazoo, Michigan, is thought to be the first city to have created such a mall in 1959. One study counted sixty-five pedestrian malls and plazas completed in the United States by 1976 (Brambilla et al. 1977). Forty-five were built after 1969, two-thirds of which were in cities with populations under 100,000 people. Approximately fifty-six percent were in cities in the Snowbelt region of the country. Outdoor malls are still being constructed. New Brunswick (New Jersey) is building a semi-pedestrian mall, and Portland, Oregon, has a transit mall underway.

Emphasis has shifted to enclosed shopping malls, a tactic which further enhances the similarity to and, thus, competitiveness with the suburban shopping mall. Protection of shoppers from the weather and use of 'magnets' or 'anchor' stores to entice consumers are lessons learned from the suburban experience, now incorporated into urban projects (Gruen and Smith 1960). Some of these enclosed malls are free-standing such

FIGURE 4 ETON CENTER, TORONTO (courtesy of Damaris Rose)

as the Galleria in Philadelphia, the Atrium in Troy, New York, or Toronto's Eton Center (Figure 4). Other malls involve the adaptive reuse of historic buildings (The Arcade in Providence and Faneuil Hall Marketplace in Boston), while others exploit unique aspects of the city such as a waterfront (Harborplace in Baltimore). Larger building complexes with offices or luxury apartments are built adjacent to or above the mall, thus bringing potential consumers into closer proximity. Examples include the shopping mall in Detroit's Renaissance Center, Worcester Center, Atlanta's Peachtree Plaza, and Pittsfield's Berkshire Common. By interspersing restaurant and fast-food establishments among the stores and by providing events to attract people to the mall, even more amenities are provided. If successful, the consumer dollar flows back into the CBD.

A second major component of CBD commercial redevelopment is the office building. Without such structures, firms will not remain or locate in the city. Buildings whose novelty and proximity to major redevelopment gives them their attractiveness can capture the types of professional and business firms which make the CBD a service, financial, and administrative center. In turn, jobs for middle-class city residents (and for some suburbanites) will be generated along with clerical and service jobs for the working class. When office buildings constitute the headquarters for banks (Bank of America in San Francisco) or corporations (PPG in Pittsburgh), the image conveyed is one of stability and progress. Large office complexes, epitomized by Detroit's Renaissance Center — four office towers containing two and one-half million square feet of office space (Figure 5) — are increasingly constructed as the centerpiece of a city's revival (Groton 1979). Rochester (New York), Los Angeles, Newark, Denver, Wilmington, and New York are a few of the many cities in which downtown redevelopment schemes contain major office buildings (U.S. Department of Housing and Urban Development 1980:3-12).

Convention centers and sports arenas are highly visible components of some redevelopment schemes. Constructed with parking garages and accessible to hotels, their purpose is to attract tourists, conventioneers, and sports fans. Once in the downtown, people will purchase food, lodging, souvenirs, and other items, thus increasing sales tax revenues. Conventions are particularly desirable. They bring money into the city without a corresponding demand for extensive public services. Because conventions are becoming more frequent, many cities are developing such facilities (Judd 1979:359-85). By attracting conventions, the city gains additional publicity which, in turn, attracts other meetings, people, and investments. Thus many cities' urban redevelopment schemes focus on upgrading old or providing new convention centers. Cities such as Baltimore, Pittsburgh, Portland (Maine), San Francisco, Washington, New York, and Long Beach have recently built or are currently building convention facilities. In 1972, ". . . seventy cities ranging in size from Pontiac, Michigan to New York City had recently opened, had under construction, or had planned multi-million dollar convention centers . . ." (Judd 1979:376).

To attract conventioneers and tourists, the city must provide the appropriate number and type of hotel spaces. In Boston, Atlanta, San Francisco, Baltimore, Long Beach, Stamford, and Denver, major new hotels are being built in downtown areas. Often these hotels are integrated physically with parking garages, shopping malls, or convention centers and may be close to new theaters, museums, or concert halls.

Downtown sports arenas have been constructed in Providence, Indianapolis, Denver, Detroit and Hartford. Even though spectators might spend less than conventioneers, the number of people who attend such events and their purchases do contribute to the city's economy. In addition, successful sports teams create an identification with the city and enhance its image (Meyer 1979).

The cultural component of redevelopment is not neglected in some cities. The Boston theater district was undergoing a renaissance in 1980 and 1981; a new museum was constructed in San Antonio; San Francisco opened a concert hall in 1981; Rochester formed a new cultural district; and Salt Lake City's symphony hall and art center opened in 1979. These specialized activities make the city unique within its region, attracting non-residents into the city and making city residence more glamorous and sophisticated.

As the city becomes more attractive and jobs are created, the hypothesis is that middle-class residents will remain and new households will move into the city. The belief is that ". . . nothing is going to ensure the rejuvenation of downtown so much as the return of the middle and upper classes as shoppers, users, and residents" (Sutton

FIGURE 5   RENAISSANCE CENTER, DETROIT (courtesy of Ford Motor Land Development Corporation)

1980:15). These people demand high quality, luxury housing within neighborhoods which provide specialty shops, cultural activities, and recreation. Some of this new housing becomes available in gentrifying neighborhoods. In the CBD a nighttime population will not only use the facilities but also make the area less foreboding to out-of-town visitors. Thus many CBD projects include luxury housing, usually in the form of high-rise apartment buildings or low-rise, townhouse developments. Jersey City's Montgomery Gateway Project includes the rehabilitation of nearly four hundred dwelling units and the construction of almost 150 townhouses. St. Paul's Lowertown redevelopment contains new medium- and high-density apartment buildings, and Boston's waterfront warehouses have been converted to dwellings. Luxury apartment buildings do not appear in all redevelopment schemes, but they are usually constructed by other developers soon after major projects are begun.

Government centers are not common in CBD redevelopment. Many cities already have adequate city halls and government buildings or are unable to finance new ones. Since its completion in the late Sixties, the Boston City Hall has become the focal point for new commercial and office activities. A few cities have made similar decisions. Wilmington's Custom House Square and San Bernadino's city hall have been used as key components of downtown urban revitalization. For the most part, however, government centers are not included in the modal commercial redevelopment project.

Consequences of CBD Redevelopment

The consequences of commercial redevelopment schemes have yet to be thoroughly studied, although some good preliminary analyses have been reported (Hartman and Kessler 1978; Stone 1976). Commercial projects do seem to provide the city with a new image and entice shoppers, theatergoers, conventioneers, tourists, and even residents to the CBD. Certain cities — Baltimore — seem to be re-establishing their regional dominance. Employment and population loss has abated in some cases — Boston, Jersey City — but many cities continue to face fiscal crises.

Certainly, redevelopment schemes remove undesirable, blighted areas and replace them with a renewed built environment. In most cases, this replacement requires the displacement of marginal businesses and lower-class residents (particularly elderly and minorities) from the transition zones targeted for redevelopment. The economic, social and psychological costs of displacement are only partially compensated by governmental payments. Businesses displaced (a shoe repair shop or neighborhood bar) are seldom welcomed into the new shopping mall and displaced residents are often unable to afford new luxury apartments. The result is a changing population and mix of services in the central business district. To a certain extent, the area is 'sanitized' of the lower and working class, with the exception of service employees in hotels, restaurants, and stores.

New ratables and job generation, seemingly positive consequences, deserve scrutiny. The city government's extraction of tax revenues from new buildings is diminished by its provision of tax abatements, increased expenditures on redevelopment infrastructure, and expanded public services for new activities (Clement 1981; Hartman 1974: 158-93). Many jobs generated in office buildings are taken by suburbanites. In San Francisco, for example, "[w]ell over 90 percent of all new white-collar jobs . . . are going to commuters" (Hartman and Kessler 1978:168). Employment in the department stores, hotels, restaurants, and convention facilities is often low-paying and lacks opportunity for advancement (Jacobs and Roistecher 1980: 354). This employment does not allow for major economic mobility. Also, jobs displaced by the initial clearance of the site moderate the apparent increase in employment.

CBD redevelopment creates increased non-public control over the central business district. Large financial institutions, corporations, and developers control the new built environment and strongly influence the activities provided. These activities, in turn, are integrated into a more tightly controlled and less eclectic urban landscape. The CBD becomes less accessible to the working and lower classes, and serves few of their needs.

Neighborhood Commercial Redevelopment

Neighborhood commercial redevelopment is part of a larger strategy of neighborhood economic development (Prattner and Mittelstadt 1973; Reuss 1979). The latter includes not only commercial redevelopment but also the creation of jobs for neighborhood residents and residential rehabilitation. This more general perspective points out the interrelationship of residential change and the viability of a neighborhood's commercial area. Just as the central business district is dependent for its success upon city-wide and metropolitan trends in population, tax base, and employment, retailers in a neighborhood commercial district must be responsive to more localized versions of these phenomena. Commercial districts serve the neighborhood's residents, for the most part, and "[a]s the neighborhood goes, so goes its shopping area" (Cassidy 1980:269).

The process and results of neighborhood commercial redevelopment differ between gentrifying neighborhoods and those undergoing incumbent upgrading. Under gentrification, new, affluent middle-class households supplant a working-class population; gourmet food shops replace general grocery stores; specialty shops ranging from clothing boutiques to plant stores are established, and new restaurants cater to more expensive tastes. This process is obvious in commercial districts as diverse as Columbus Avenue on the upper West Side of Manhattan, Castro Street in San Francisco, and Little Five Points in Atlanta (Chernoff 1980).

In neighborhoods undergoing incumbent upgrading, there is an attempt by merchants' associations and local governmental agencies to retain and strengthen existing businesses and, thus, preserve and enhance the present mix of services. Physical improvements are less drastic, for example, than in gentrifying neighborhoods. Historic preservation is a minor theme. In addition, more governmental assistance is involved. HUD's Office of Neighborhood Development, the Neighborhood Reinvestment Corporation, the Small Business Administration's Office of Business Revitalization, and many city economic development agencies engage in neighborhood commercial redevelopment. During 1977-1978, the Office of Business Revitalization, along with HUD and the Economic Development Administration (EDA) operated demonstration projects in twenty-five cities to show the potential for such neighborhood commercial upgrading (Subcommittee on Capital, Investment and Business Opportunities 1978). Neighborhood commercial redevelopment in areas of incumbent revitalization constitutes our focus. Very little research has been done on the gentrification of neighborhood shopping areas.

Problems and Solutions

Older commercial areas in inner-city neighborhoods suffer from various obstacles to revitalization (Goldstein and Davis 1977; Levatino 1978). The neighborhood has experienced a diminution in local household income and, thus, purchasing power. Buildings in the commercial district have deteriorated; vandalism has become more frequent; the number of marginal businesses has increased; and the variety of services provided has decreased. Developed prior to the era of the automobile, these local commercial areas usually lack parking facilities, which weakens their ability to compete with suburban commerical districts. With the demise of businesses, the focus of the commercial area is fragmented. Thriving businesses, marginal ones, and vacant storefronts are intermixed. No concentration of businesses exists to attract shoppers. As crime increases, people are less likely to visit the area, particularly at night. Thus stores close after sundown, which further exacerbates the perception of danger. The scarcity of reinvestment funds and insurance company redlining makes reversal of decline very difficult (National Commission on Neighborhoods 1979:37).[8]

Neighborhood commercial redevelopment entails physical renovation and economic revitalization of the district's businesses. Renovation includes the rehabilitation of storefronts and interiors, public improvements to the shopping street, expanded

---

[8]Insurance redlining is the illegal practice of refusing contracts in areas evaluated by insurance companies as too risky for profitable insurance protection (*see* Dingemans 1979).

parking facilities, and a variety of other activities directed toward making the area an attractive, accessible, pleasant place in which to browse and purchase. For some, this is the most important factor in the revitalization of a commercial center (Levatino 1978:32). Just as the redevelopment of the CBD utilizes a 'new' and vibrant physical environment to attract people, a similar striving for a pleasant and enticing atmosphere is part of neighborhood commercial redevelopment. Economic revitalization, on the other hand, requires that the commercial district's mix of businesses be adjusted to the consumer demands within its market area, that merchants be assisted in buying and displaying goods, and that attempts be made to publicize the shopping area and entice consumers.

Among reported examples of such neighborhood commercial redevelopment are St. Johns Business District in Portland, Oregon, and York Road in Baltimore (Neighborhood Reinvestment Corporation, n.d.); River East in Toledo, Bedford Stuyvesant in New York, Atwells Avenue in Providence, and Brightwood Memorial Square in Springfield, Massachusetts (National Commission on Neighborhoods 1979:148-55); Federal Hill in Providence (Williams 1978); and the Cross Street Marketplace in Baltimore (U.S. Department of Housing and Urban Development 1979b:50-55). In New York, over thirty commercial districts are being assisted by the city's Office of Neighborhood Economic Development (New York City, Office of Economic Development, n.d.). The major emphasis in all of these commercial redevelopment efforts is physical rehabilitation.

In some cities physical improvements focus on the creation of a pedestrian mall with plantings, street furniture, paving, and other outdoor amenities. In most cases, the physical upgrading is less bold; storefronts, signs, and public facilities are improved. This usually means the imposition of design standards for facades to make the district's visual displays consistent and replace the garish signs and storefronts which typify declining commercial districts. Public improvements include provision of more parking, repaving sidewalks and streets, planting trees, improving street lighting, developing vacant lots into mini-parks, strengthening code enforcement, and removing dilapidated structures. The objective is to develop an identity and visual unity for the shopping area to make it more attractive. In some cities, notably New York and Philadelphia, the government purchases vacant stores and develops 'shopsteading' programs through which local merchants can buy stores at low prices if they rehabilitate and operate them.

For physical redevelopment to have the proper effect, attention must also be given to the economic viability of the businesses in the shopping area. "In any neighborhood where there are concentrations of population, there is automatically a retail market potential" (Goldstein and Davis 1977:30). Commercial establishments must capture a higher percentage of the retail dollars from their potential market area. The shopping area may never provide the array of specialty items available in the CBD or the major durables (appliances) stocked by downtown and suburban department stores, but it must meet the needs of neighborhood residents and not allow their purchases of non-specialty items and non-durables to be diverted to suburban malls or other neighborhood commercial districts.

The first step is a market analysis to ascertain the market area of the shopping district, the disposable income of the residents within that area, the types of goods and services they desire, the attributes which attract them to commercial areas, their perceptions of the problems and prospects for the commercial district, and the locational strength of the competition (W. Cox 1969; Forbes 1977). With this information, a variety of decisions is possible. One is whether or not to pursue a major department store or supermarket to 'anchor' the commercial district. Another is to attract stores, currently missing from the mix of establishments, which will capture a presently untapped portion of the market. Market analyses also enable local governmental agencies and other organizations (such as merchant associations) to provide appropriate technical assistance and management counseling to neighborhood businesses. They may determine the appropriate mix of goods, marketing, advertising, and suitable management techniques. These organizations may suggest events to attract shoppers and changes in the physical environment which will alter perceptions. Merchants and local police might collaborate on programs (more frequent patrols or better alarm systems) to make the area safer.

Some physical improvements and adjustments in business practices might be funded through govermental sources. However, merchants must obtain private and public financing for their operations. One approach is for the merchants to band together and establish a special assessment district. Each then contributes an amount to the overall costs of redevelopment proportional to expected benefits. This benefit is usually measured by the location of the business relative to the center of the district and its proximity to physical improvements, such as a central plaza. Another approach is through government loans and grants. HUD, SBA and EDA, as well as local offices of economic and community development, disburse property rehabilitation loans and grants, monies for operating loans, and even equity capital for starting small businesses. Some of these agencies also provide technical assistance. In addition, merchants, individually or collectively, often approach local banks to convince them of the benefits of lending money for commercial redevelopment. Loans and the resultant changes, it might be argued, will stabilize the neighborhood and insulate existing residential and commercial loans from default. Without the infusion of governmental and private capital, however, the redevelopment of neighborhood commercial districts will not occur.

The strategy for implementing physical and economic revitalization is similar from one neighborhood commercial redevelopment effort to the next (Goldstein 1977). The model, propounded by the Neighborhood Reinvestment Corporation, pivots upon a private-public partnership among the area's merchants, governmental agencies, local financial institutions, and, sometimes, residents of the neighborhood (Stout and Otteson 1980). The premise is that ". . . if reinvestment is to achieve both private and public investment goals, a partnership is necessary . . ." (Neighborhood Reinvestment Corporation n.d.:1). To be successful, the partnership must be directed by an organization which can undertake studies, develop plans, and coordinate activities. This might be a merchant's association, a local development corporation (Daniel 1977), or a government agency. Its goal is to replicate the function of a management firm in a suburban shopping mall (Cassidy 1980:280). Without a formal organization, actions to upgrade the commercial district will remain fragmented and may not be mutually supportive.

Each participant has certain obligations to the partnership. For merchants, these include the commitment to remain in the neighborhood, to reinvest, and to work with the district's organization. Local government should engage in technical assistance, provide local and intergovernmental funding, and undertake public improvements. Local banks are requested to make loans to businesses and residents in the neighborhood so that disinvestment does not occur. But most importantly, neighborhood residents must be convinced to shop in the district, use its services, and attend local events. If these activities are successful, and each participant group fulfills its obligations, then the commercial district will move along the revitalization path.

The consequences of successful upgrading of non-gentrified, neighborhood commercial districts are that shoppers patronize the stores, retail sales increase, profits rise, the neighborhood is stabilized, some new jobs are generated, and tax revenues expand. This occurs because a larger share of the local consumer dollar has been captured and because the market area for the commercial district has been expanded as a result of increased accessibility and appeal (Goldstein and Davis 1977: 198). The physical environment is improved, and shopping is now safe, lively, and attractive.

Prospects for Commercial Revitalization

In our description and analysis of commercial redevelopment, both CBD and neighborhood levels have been treated as if they are independent of a larger metropolitan context. Furthermore, the interrelationship between CBD and neighborhood commercial revitalization was not addressed. Each issue deserves brief comment.

CBD revitalization has goals related to past glory and suburban competition. Since the population of revitalizing cities is generally stable or shrinking, achieving a former scale of commercial development is unlikely. It is also unlikely that the city's CBD will make much headway against competition with the suburban shopping malls, not to mention the central commercial districts of inner-ring suburbs. Certainly, the CBD can regain a particular attraction for specific population groups, as Boston, San Francisco, Baltimore, and Manhattan have demonstrated. However, the 'back to the city' movement is small, and the fastest population growth is now non-metropolitan. The CBD might well become a more specialized commercial, cultural, and recreational area with regional attraction. Many of its less specialized functions, however, will continue to be duplicated in the suburbs.

Neighborhood commercial redevelopment is not a phenomenon occurring simultaneously in all areas within a single city. Residential areas undergoing gentrification and incumbent upgrading have such activities, but many other mixed-use, declining, and abandoned neighborhoods do not. Resources are being selectively applied. Thus, neighborhood commercial revitalization exhibits an uneven pattern across the urban landscape. In fact, successful commercial redevelopment in one neighborhood might capture shoppers from adjacent neighborhoods, further contributing to their commercial demise. One might hope for a distribution of retail activities such that each neighborhood contains a viable and stable commercial district. Such a pattern is unlikely, because affluent, successful enterprises attract more capital and consumers.

The relationship between CBD commercial redevelopment and that in the neighborhoods has not been adequately researched. In theory, regional and local commercial areas should form a mutually supportive hierarchy, neither competing with the other. This is not the case in reality. Most obvious are those neighborhood commercial districts in close proximity to the CBD which might lose their neighborhood character because of the spillover of more specialized activities. CBD and neighborhood also compete for private capital to fund redevelopment. Not without limit, funds may be siphoned off by major CBD developers. Moreover, government expertise and attention is scarce and politically controlled. Thus, while CBD and neighborhood commercial redevelopment seem to be distinct, if not complementary, processes, a little probing unearths interesting and important competitive dimensions.

5

Residential Revitalization

The renovation of inner-city housing and the rehabilitation of urban neighborhoods is the second major component of urban revitalization. It is also a most fascinating geographic phenomenon, involving transformations of the built, and often the social, environment. Many city neighborhoods, after decades of decline and disinvestment, are now experiencing rehabilitation, new construction, and rising property values. Conventional theories of neighborhood change, predicting an inexorable deterioration of residential areas, have been violated.

The neighborhoods of revitalizing cities are diverse. In a relatively large city like Boston or New Orleans, neighborhoods with well-maintained housing, clean streets, few social problems, and affluent occupants exist within walking distance of blocks that are all but abandoned. Investment has ceased, buildings are empty, arson occurs frequently, and the residents are socially and economically disadvantaged. In between these two extremes are neighborhoods with different degrees of growth or decay, investment or disinvestment, affluence or poverty, high or low quality public services, and standard or dilapidated housing.

Residential revitalization takes place in only certain of these neighborhoods. Two contrasting processes are at work. They differ with the character of the neighborhood at both the beginning and at the culmination of renovation and involve quite different populations. The first process is termed 'gentrification.' Middle- and upper-income people move into a neighborhood, renovate housing, and displace the previous inhabitants. The alternative, 'incumbent upgrading,' occurs when residents of a neighborhood stay and invest their money and effort in refurbishing their homes.

Both forms of neighborhood revitalization reflect larger trends. One of these is increasing government interest in neighborhood development since the Urban Renewal program. Many new planning procedures were introduced in response to the CBD bias of Urban Renewal and to its tendency toward large scale clearance rather than preservation of existing neighborhoods (Committee on Banking, Housing and Urban Affairs 1973: 39-67). Programs, such as Model Cities and CDBG, and policies, such as the Community Reinvestment Act, have been created to deal with the problems facing urban neighborhoods (Schoenberg and Rosenbaum 1980: 13-29). Since the Sixties, neighborhoods have also taken on heightened political meaning (Goering 1979; Levy 1979). Model Cities and the War on Poverty focused attention on the

FIGURE 6   HOUSING ABANDONMENT ADJACENT TO A
GENTRIFYING NEIGHBORHOOD, BALTIMORE (photograph
by Robert A. Beauregard)

poverty areas of cities; community control emerged as an important movement (Fainstein and Fainstein 1974). Many ethnic groups followed the lead of Blacks and organized into neighborhood associations. Neighborhoods became important elements in the delivery of public services with neighborhood empowerment as a central theme. Gentrification and incumbent upgrading are descendents of these movements.

Gentrification

The term 'gentrification' is attributed to Ruth Glass who described a process occurring in London in the early 1960's. Shabby, working-class mews were acquired by middle-class people who converted them to elegant and expensive homes (N. Smith 1979: 25). Because the word 'gentry' implies a land-owning aristocracy, 'gentrification' may be etymologically inappropriate to describe what now happens in North American cities. Nevertheless, it has acquired widespread and popular acceptance (London 1980: 77-8). Gentrification occurs when there is a substantial replacement of a neighborhood's residents with newcomers who are of higher income and who, having acquired homes cheaply, renovate them and upgrade the neighborhood (Figures 6 and 7).

Gentrification is an aspect of urban revitalization which has received considerable attention in both the popular and professional literature. When perceived, somewhat erroneously, as a migration back to the city by middle- and upper-middle income people, it is interpreted as a vote of confidence which carries hope for urban revival. As such, it reverses a long-term trend in which a move up the socioeconomic scale meant a move outward from the city center towards the outer suburbs. However, the concomitant displacement of lower-income and working-class people from gentrifying neighborhoods

FIGURE 7   REHABILITATED HOUSING IN A GENTRIFIED NEIGHBORHOOD, BALTIMORE (photograph by Robert A. Beauregard)

has likewise generated considerable literature (Goodman and Shain 1980; London 1980). Geographers have contributed significantly to the description and analysis of gentrification by exploring the spatial aspects of its causes and consequences and by offering new theoretical explanations of its occurrence (Cybriwsky 1978, 1980; Ford 1976; Ford and Fusch 1978; Fusch 1980; Hodge 1980; Lauria 1980; Ley 1980, 1981; Ley and Mercer 1980; O'Loughlin and Munski 1979; N. Smith 1979a, 1979b, 1981; Winters 1979).

We have no single, reliable measure of the extent of residential revitalization, and data on such indicators as increasing house values, home-improvement expenditures, or changes in household incomes within a neighborhood do not allow disaggregation of incumbent upgrading and gentrification. Numerous case studies and surveys (Black 1980; Lipton 1980) suggest that gentrification is occuring in one or two neighborhoods in many cities, and some larger cities have several such neighborhoods. Gentrifying neighborhoods are reported, among other places, in the Washington areas of Capitol Hill and Mount Pleasant (Gale 1979, 1980), Boston's South End (Auger 1979), Baltimore (Gasser 1979), Philadelphia's Queen Village and Society Hill (Levy 1978; Levy and Cybriwsky 1980; N. Smith 1979a; 1979b), New Orleans (Laska and Spain 1979, 1980), Columbus's German Village (Fusch 1980), Charleston (Tournier 1980), Seattle (Hodge 1980), and Vancouver (Ley 1980). New York City has numerous neighborhoods, such as Park Slope in Brooklyn or the Upper West Side of Manhattan, into which middle-income professionals are moving, sometimes into converted industrial buildings, and from which the poor are displaced (Bergman 1979; Winters 1979). Gentrification occurs with less publicity and on a less spectacular scale in many other cities.

The quintessential gentrifying neighborhood is small, usually restricted to a few blocks. However, its "image and importance often exceed [its] true size" (Clay 1979:17). It is frequently within a mile of the central business district, typically on a hill or waterfront, near a significant open space, or adjacent to or part of an area of historic interest (Clay 1980: 20-22). Most gentrifying neighborhoods are in areas of mixed land use, close to retail, commercial, or government foci, but not near public housing projects (Clay 1979:21). A survey of residential revitalization in the thirty largest cities of the United States found that gentrifying neighborhoods are, on the average, much older than those with incumbent upgrading; ". . . 46 percent of the gentrified neighborhoods compared to only 11 percent of the upgrading neighborhoods are at least 100 years old" (Clay 1980: 21). Given the attraction of historic sites, and more central location, such age is not unexpected.

Typically, buildings in these neighborhoods are structurally sound, despite their age, and often have architectural or aesthetic interest. Clay (1979:18) found that a majority of gentrifying neighborhoods had low residential density, with one-family or two-family structures. However, there are significant exceptions to this generalization. In New York, five story tenements in the East Village have been converted to expensive apartments (Goldstein, 1980), while Columbia University is currently renovating single-room occupancy (SRO) hotels and low-income apartment buildings on the Upper West Side (Keating 1980a). In many cities, houses built several generations ago for large middle-class families have also been converted for residential use by two or three small, affluent, professional families. Industrial warehouses and factories are being remodelled into condominiums and townhouses in older industrial cities such as Paterson, New Jersey. Brick sidewalks, gas lamps, and wrought iron complete the landscape transformations in many instances (Benefit Street in Providence and Larimer Square in Denver).

Gentrification is primarily a private sector process. The role of government is less overt than in other forms of urban redevelopment, but it is by no means absent. Government assists and encourages gentrification by providing grants and loans for housing rehabilitation to eligible households, declaring historic districts and landmarks, improving public services, and making public capital investments such as a sewerage system or park improvements. Government further stimulates renovation through strict code enforcement and by allocating monies from sources such as Community Development Block Grants to these local areas. The federal government strongly encourages home ownership through tax concessions as well as subsidized low interest loans for historic preservation and for energy-conserving renovation. Increases in property tax assessments, moreover, speed the flight of original residents and free more housing for gentrifiers.

The Gentrifiers

Gentrification is often heralded as a migration back to the city by disillusioned suburbanites. In fact, most people moving into gentrifying neighborhoods come from other parts of the city rather than from the suburbs. Gale (1979: 296) reported that less than twenty percent of the resettlers surveyed in the gentrifying neighborhoods of Atlanta, Boston, Washington, and Cambridge said that they had moved from the suburbs. Laska and Spain (1980:119) found the same percentage in New Orleans. In Society Hill in Philadelphia, only fourteen percent were previously suburbanites (N. Smith 1979b: 540). These data suggest that affluent suburbanites are not returning to the cities with their investments, consumer demands, and tax revenues — a migration which could stimulate the urban economy. It may be, rather, that many gentrifiers are would-be suburbanites priced out of the suburbs who have turned to other neighborhoods within the city. Commonly, they invest both capital and 'sweat equity' in the renovation of their homes. Thus, while they reinvest in the city, they do not add to its population. While such neighborhood resettlement nonetheless retains middle class residents, it does not reverse the major suburban migration of preceding decades.

The gentrifying resettlers are typically young singles and couples without children. Most families with children have only one or two. In the Capitol Hill area in Washington, only 21 percent of households had children, and most of the few children of school age were enrolled in private schools (Gale 180: 98). There are exceptions; in a gentrifying neighborhood of New Orleans, 62 percent of households had children. Still, 90 percent of them attended private schools (Laska and Spain 1980: 119). Most heads of households are professionals under 45 (Clay 1980: 21). Less than fifteen percent of the U.S. population over 25 years of age have four year college degrees, yet surveys in gentrifying neighborhoods show that in Atlanta 62 percent of household heads have college degrees, in St. Paul 80 percent, and, in one Washington neighborhood, 97 percent! In this last neighborhood, moreover, 87 percent had graduate degrees (Gale 1979: 294). Racially, most immigrants to gentrifying neighborhoods are White, although a very few areas experiencing rejuvenation show an influx of the Black middle class (Strivers Row in Harlem and parts of Bedford-Stuyvesant in Brooklyn; Winters 1979:14).

Whether residential revitalization increases or decreases socioeconomic homogeneity is an interesting question. While a return of middle-class people to the inner city might increase heterogeneity, the numbers returning are very small. Those moving within the city frequently search out economically and ethnically diverse neighborhoods (Allen 1980; Weiler 1978). Gentrified neighborhoods, however, remain socioeconomically and racially mixed only for a few transitional years. Ultimately they become ". . . as socioeconomically homogeneous as most suburban neighborhoods" (Fusch 1980:169). In New Orleans, Annapolis, Georgetown (Newsom 1971), and Charleston, the displacement of Blacks by Whites has simply changed the form of segregation (Tournier 1980:183). Hodge (1980:199) found that in two gentrifying neighborhoods in Seattle, segregation occurred *within* a seemingly integrated neighborhood. Gentrified neighborhoods become homogeneous by class, race, and even age. The elderly are displaced, and certain types of families are discouraged from living there. In neighborhoods such as Queen Village in Philadelphia, families with children ". . . frequently find themselves with inadequate or no yard space for their children to play in" (Weiler 1980: 226).

The Dynamics of Gentrification

How does the process of gentrification start and progress towards complete neighborhood renovation (Figure 8)? Prior to the beginning of resettlement these neighborhoods have usually experienced decades of decline with minimal investment in the upkeep of buildings or of the surrounding physical environment. Some have reached a stage in which abandonment is rife and shells of formerly gracious homes are boarded up. Others retain a stable, working-class residential population. In some neighborhoods the 'urban pioneers' buy homes cheaply, renovate, and live in them. Gale (1980: 103) reported that the earlier buyers in Capitol Hill were often single males, while Clay (1979: 17) wrote that "many observers mentioned the significant presence in the early stages of homosexuals and design professionals." Many are initially attracted by low prices and tolerance of unconventional life-styles, rather than by the opportunity eventually to realize large profits. London and some cities in the United States have development companies or real estate agents who buy many properties, or even whole blocks, in a neighborhood. In Washington, a kind of 'reverse block-busting' occurred when real estate speculators searched out likely properties in the path of the wave of restoration and made attractive offers for the property. If the owner was reluctant to sell, costly repairs required by a cooperative building inspector could be persuasive (Richards and Rowe 1977).

A National Urban Coalition study (1978) of sixty-five neighborhoods in forty-four cities found that after an initial investment period of a few years, a second period of intense investment follows during which the physical quality of the neighborhood changes dramatically. Property values of both renovated houses and of shells requiring complete rehabilitation increase rapidly. In 1978, renovated homes were selling for $100,000 in Washington, $175,000 to $200,000 in San Francisco, and $150,000 in New Orleans (National Urban Coalition 1978: 5). Houses purchased for $21,000 in Columbus's Victorian Village were marked up 400 percent after renovation. Price changes in most gentrifying neighborhoods can be very rapid. A building in the East Village of New York was sold for $33,000 one year and $75,000 the next — without renovation (Goldstein 1980: 18). Rents are not immune from this phenomenon. Typical studio apartment rents in Long Island City, New York, increased from $200 to $800 a month in a couple of years (Keating 1980b: 24).

In some neighborhoods the speculation is particularly intense as the same buildings are bought and sold for a large profit, sometimes over one hundred percent, within the space of a few months. Such a process is called 'flipping.' In a two year period in the

FIGURE 8   GENTRIFICATION BY DOONESBURY
(Copyright 1980 by G. B. Trudeau. Reprinted with permission
of Universal Press Syndicate)

early Seventies in Washington, twenty-one percent of all recorded sales of row and semi-detached homes and flats involved two or more sales of the same property. Nearly seventy percent of these sales were concentrated in only five neighborhoods (Richards and Rowe 1977: 54).

Apart from the large profits to be made, another striking aspect of gentrification is the speed with which such neighborhoods change. While it typically takes decades of slow decline for a neighborhood to reach the stage prior to gentrification, only two years are necessary to reverse the trend. In addition, reinvestment seems to diffuse contagiously. O'Loughlin and Munski (1979:68) have documented this process for New Orleans, showing that clusters of renovated properties eventually coalesce as preservation gains momentum.

At a more advanced stage of revival, the neighborhood attracts buyers less by the low prices characteristic of an earlier stage than by new amenities and the opportunity for a secure investment. Although no evidence suggests that gentrification has reversed in any neighborhood where it had started, the process is still young and, furthermore, unsuccessful attempts are seldom recorded (Clay 1979:17). The original pioneers obviously take greater risks, but have less to lose. After the neighborhood has been partially revitalized and, most importantly, discovered by the communications media, the second stage resettlers who buy or rent are more often professionals. The second wave is often less tolerant of class and cultural differences between themselves and the indigenous inhabitants and more concerned about increasing the value of their property. New residents often work to organize the neighborhood around such issues as historic designation or the improvement of public services. During this period displacement of original residents is most severe.

In the third, mature stage, the neighborhood transformation is virtually complete. Most buildings are renovated and few bargains remain. Local government has recognized the neighborhood organization and upgraded local services. New developments which threaten the character of the neighborhood are opposed by its middle class residents. The neighborhood is stabilized and gentrification complete.

The Displaced

The major social and geographical issue raised by gentrification is that of displacement of the original residents and small businesses by more affluent households and by businesses more attuned to their consumption patterns. There is no single satisfactory definition of displacement. The most commonly used is that of Grier and Grier (1978: 8):

> *Displacement occurs when any household is forced to move from its residence by conditions which affect the dwelling or its immediate surroundings, and which:*
> *1. are beyond the household's reasonable ability to control or prevent;*
> *2. occur despite the household's having met all previously imposed conditions of occupancy; and*
> *3. make continued occupancy by that household impossible, hazardous, or unaffordable.*

The scale of displacement varies from relatively few households in a neighborhood which has previously experienced widespread abandonment (such a situation is unusual) to major out-migration in densely populated, inner-city areas. Estimates of the number of households displaced by gentrification vary widely, and accurate accounting is impossible. Direct displacement occurs when homes are acquired through eminent domain or when rental leases terminate and are not renewed. More residents suffer indirect displacement through rising rents and property taxes, increased living costs, and by unofficial harassment by landlords seeking to empty a building prior to its sale or rehabilitation.

A study of the largest fourteen cities of the United States found that, in most, the total number of households directly displaced annually by gentrification was less than two hundred. However, in selected cities, such as Washington and San Francisco, the problem was much greater and several thousand households were displaced each year (Grier and Grier 1978). A National Urban Coalition study (1978) found that while forty-five percent of neighborhoods had blue collar residents prior to gentrification, only fifteen percent did afterwards. The *Annual Housing Survey* estimates that approximately eighty-six percent of the 500,000 U.S. households are displaced each year through private action, but it does not provide a disaggregation which would distinguish gentrifying neighborhoods from other neighborhoods with residential mobility (Meek 1978: 3). A report on displacement issued by HUD in 1979 and various articles by Howard Sumka (1979, 1980a, 1980b), a Deputy Director of the Division of Community Research at HUD, suggest that displacement is not a major problem and, while it hurts some, it is a cost which is more than balanced by the benefits of neighborhood revival. That evaluation has been criticized by others who point out that HUD's own figures can be interpreted to mean that over half a million households are displaced annually (Hartman 1979b). In addition, the data used by HUD in its *Annual Housing Survey* and the *Current Population Survey* may be inappropriate for measuring the extent of displacement (Kotler 1980: 33). In 1981, HUD reported in *Housing Affairs Letter* that it regarded private market displacement as a local, rather than a national, phenomenon, and that it would undertake no further studies on this aspect of displacement. However, in a carefully reasoned analysis of existing studies and data, LeGates and Hartman (1981) calculated that if all forms of displacement are included, 2.5 million persons a year would be a *conservative* estimate of all involuntary moves, including those resulting from gentrification.

There is more agreement on the question of who is displaced. Study after study has found that minorities, elderly, and low-income people generally are displaced in disproportionate numbers. Since 1976, for example, 2,000 Hispanic familes have been displaced by commercial and residential revitalization in Atlantic City, New Jersey (Perez, Garza, and Fulco 1980). New residents met strong resistance from displaced Puerto Ricans in Philadelphia's Spring Garden neighborhood (National Urban Coalition 1978:19). Blacks have been displaced from gentrifying neighborhoods in Baltimore (Quayle 1980), Washington (Gale 1980; Richards and Rowe 1977), and other cities (Clay 1980; Long 1980:71; Spain 1980:33).

The low-income elderly often form a significant proportion of the original population and are particularly vulnerable to increased living costs characteristic of gentrifying neighborhoods (Myers 1978). They are typically long-term residents. As tenants they cannot afford rising rents. As homeowners, they are burdened by a spurt in property values and the additional taxes that follow. Renovation costs, particularly if the house is in a designated historic district requiring period materials and techniques, exceed their budgets. Almost eighty percent of the neighborhoods studied in the National Urban Coalition Survey (1978:7) reported a decline in the number of elderly residents after rehabilitation. In a 1975 study of apartments converted to condominiums in Washington, forty-five percent of the displaced were elderly and two-thirds had yearly incomes under $15,000. "Slightly over half of these households responded that they chose to move rather than to purchase their apartment because it would have been too expensive to stay" (Cincin-Sain 1980:71).

Renters are usually the first to leave. Of those neighborhoods surveyed by the National Urban Coalition (1978: 8) which initially had a predominance of renters, about ninety-five percent showed a decrease in renters after rehabilitation. Another vulnerable group of displacees are families with more than two children, families for whom finding replacement housing is particularly difficult. If they do find housing in another neighborhood within the city, it usually means living in over-crowded conditions (Hartman 1979a).

Very few studies have been made of where the displaced move. The evidence available suggests that most people move very short distances, but that they also move several times (Cincin-Sain 1980:72). Short moves enable people to maintain proximity to employment, services, and friends, thus minimizing the social and economic costs of displacement. But the tendency to cluster close to the original location also maximizes the vulnerability to successive displacement (LeGates and Hartman 1981:227).

The costs of displacement are not only financial (moving expenses, security deposits, increased rent, new utilities) but social (loss of community ties, reduced proximity to friends and relatives and to medical and other social services) and emotional (the trauma of displacement from familiar locations). Some households obtain housing as good or better after relocation, and some homeowners are able to profit from the sale of their homes.[9] For those displaced by government or government-assisted projects, partial reimbursement of expenses is available through the Uniform Relocation and Assistance Act. However, since gentrification is primarily a private-sector phenomenon, little financial assistance appears for displacees. For a large majority of those displaced, the costs exceed the benefits (Cincin-Sain 1980) and living conditions suffer as a result of the move (Hartman 1979a).

Gentrification thus poses a dilemma for policymakers. On the one hand, they wish to attract and retain middle- and upper-income residents in the central city. Such households both demand and support a high quality of public services which can then be enjoyed by other city dwellers. The upgrading of residential districts which they provide can attract new businesses, bringing more jobs to the city. But to make room for these new residents, the poor are displaced. Rather than seeking to stop gentrification, some policymakers urge that greater effort be made to monitor the extent of displacement and to improve mitigation programs and funding. Their intent is to assist original residents to remain and renovate their homes and to help those who leave to relocate successfully (N. Smith 1979b:303; National Urban Coalition 1978:23-25). "Public policy must intervene to control or compensate for the private market externalities that displacement represents if the interests of the entire city and not just the middle class are to be protected" (Clay 1979:33).

Incumbent Upgrading

The second major process by which urban neighborhoods are being revitalized is incumbent upgrading. Such neighborhoods are typically occupied by stable, moderate-income households, usually characterized by a relatively high percentage of homeowners, and where there are signs of deterioration in both the housing stock and the general physical environment. Either with or without government assistance, residents have organized to resist the forces of decline and to reinvest in their environment. Although this process does not involve the rapid migration and landscape change of gentrification, it is socially and geographically significant (Lauria 1980).

In incumbent upgrading, local residents undertake physical improvements to their properties and the neighborhood in general, ". . . with no significant changes in the

---

[9]The estimation of profit in this case is difficult. Homeowners may sell their property for much more than its purchase price. However, the family is likely to have to pay even more for replacement housing since inflation has reduced the value of the dollar and increased mortgage costs.

socio-economic status or characteristics of the population" (Clay 1979: 7). It is a revitalization of place which, unlike gentrification, allows existing residents to remain (Downs 1979). Desiring to maintain their urban lifestyle and faced with high costs for new housing, residents select conservation of their present neighborhood over migration to the suburbs (James 1980:131). The neighborhood is stabilized physically and socially, and the impending deterioration caused by a lack of property investment and of environmental concern is halted (Levy 1980).

During the Sixties and Seventies, there was a significant increase in the formation of neighborhood organizations whose purposes included the redevelopment of the physical environment (Goering 1979; Perlman 1976). In addition, data exist which document reinvestment in central-city housing between 1970 and 1977 (James 1980). In 1977, for example, owners of single-family properties in central cities spent $3.6 billion on maintenance, repairs, and improvements. This sum constituted approximately one-fifth of the total reinvestment in such housing for the United States as a whole. These data, however, do not distinguish reinvestment in gentrifying neighborhoods from that occurring in neighborhoods engaged in incumbent upgrading. There has also been an expansion in the amount of governmental attention directed to urban neighborhoods. The major objective of CDBG, for example, is to reinvest in neighborhoods which might be suitable for incumbent upgrading. This program also allows local communities to designate certain areas for special attention under its Neighborhood Strategy Area (NSA) guidelines, but data have not been collected which document the scale of this approach to residential revitalization.

It is also difficult to characterize the geographical distribution of incumbent upgrading. As we shall see, the most likely neighborhoods can be identified (Clay 1980; Clay 1979: 44), but less is known about the type of cities in which upgrading might occur and thus about their regional distribution. Some suggestive data come from the Neighborhood Housing Services (NHS) program for incumbent upgrading sponsored by the Neighborhood Reinvestment Corporation (Neighborhood Reinvestment Corporation 1980). In late 1980, this public corporaton had 117 NHS neighborhoods in 92 cities across the United States. Most of these neighborhoods are in cities in the Northeast and Central states, over eighty percent of the neighborhoods in cities with populations greater than 100,000, and close to seventy percent of these neighborhoods in cities that lost population between 1970 and 1975. Interestingly, not one city growing in population has more than one NHS neighborhood.

Problems and Prospects

Neighborhoods engaged in incumbent upgrading confront a major but elusive threat to their existence and to the quality of their physical environments — disinvestment (Cassidy 1980: 23-49). For neighborhoods in which many of the housing units are owner-occupied, disinvestment may be caused by a combination of low incomes and reluctance on the part of financial institutions to provide loans. In fact, this latter phenomenon has received a great deal of attention by those involved in incumbent upgrading. Banks and other lending institutions, as well as insurance companies, have been accused of 'redlining,' identifying certain neighborhoods as unworthy of loans or property insurance on the basis of broad, discriminatory racial or income criteria (Dingemans 1979; Marcuse 1979; Squires *et al.* 1979). Because a neighborhood may be experiencing an influx of minority or low-income households or have an older housing stock, the lending institutions simply decide that all households in that neighborhood are bad credit risks. Thus, they withhold loans for reinvestment in housing. A self-fulfilling prophecy results. Without investment and other financial assistance, neighborhoods will inevitably deteriorate.

In the Seventies, neighborhood groups identified the redlining phenomenon and pressured financial institutions to reverse such policies. Their efforts led to legislation (such as the Home Mortgage Disclosure Act and the Community Reinvestment Act) to penalize lending institutions for such behavior and to reverse the process through 'greenlining,' redirecting monies to neighborhoods in which disinvestment had once been the norm (National Commission on Neighborhoods 1979: 65-127). Freeing funds for reinvestment attacks the predominant problem confronting these neighborhoods — deterioration of housing stock.

Neighborhoods engaged in incumbent upgrading must also have certain positive qualities which can be exploited. The presence of a moderate-income, stable residential population is important, as is owner-occupation of most homes. Environmental deterioration in only incipient stages may be a vital characteristic. The housing stock and built environment can be more easily brought back to a quality condition. Such neighborhoods usually have sound housing requiring minor improvements, rather than structurally unsound buildings needing 'gut' rehabilitation, hence lessening the funds required for revitalization.[10] Most nebulous, but probably most important, however, is the potential sense of community existing within the neighborhood. To make incumbent upgrading successful, people must organize themselves into neighborhood associations which can lobby local government to improve public services and to join in pressuring banks to loan money, entice other residents to fix up their housing, and generate a greater pride in the neighborhood.

Organizations and Activities

A neighborhood association may be government-sponsored (as is the case with those funded under the CDBG program or under numerous state programs such as the Neighborhood Preservation Program in New Jersey); it may be only indirectly tied to the government (NHS neighborhood associations are an example); or it may be totally private in the sense that the residents themselves support the organization through contributions or fund-raising (from foundations, churches, ethnic organizations, and other sources). A general strategy, similar to that championed by the Neighborhood Reinvestment Corporation, is common to all neighborhood organizations engaged in incumbent upgrading.

The NHS strategy relies heavily upon local community involvement (Albrandt and Brophy 1975: 127-50; Kuttner 1980). Once residents band together and approach the Neighborhood Reinvestment Corporation, they are given assistance in setting up a more formal organization. Major emphasis is given to the formation of a partnership among residents, leaders of local financial institutions, elected officials and agency directors, and the NHS program staff. Each has a role to play.

Residents join in neighborhood activities and improve their homes. Local bankers make loans available and set aside funds for a revolving loan fund or a high risk loan

---

[10]'Gut' rehabilitation involves the reconstruction of electrical, heating, and plumbing systems; the construction of new walls and even floors; and, sometimes, the replacement of the structural supports of the building. Moderate rehabilitation is less extensive.

pool. Local government directs CDBG and other monies to the neighborhood and improves local services, especially building code enforcement. Local government also aids in preventing displacement by sensitizing tax assessors to the financial burdens of working class households. The NHS staff coordinates these various groups and agencies and provides technical assistance and advice to neighborhood residents. It is the facilitator, bringing people together to focus on the needs of the neighborhood and to engage in activities which reverse impending deterioration.

The central activity undertaken within this strategy is, of course, the rehabilitation of housing. As the major component of the built environment, the embodiment of any perception of decline or prosperity, and a major contributor to the well-being of the residents, housing receives top priority. While external improvements, such as paint or aluminum siding, help to fuel the contagion effect by which adjacent homeowners recognize the revitalization of the neighborhood and themselves reinvest in their own housing, internal improvements (new heating or electrical systems) are equally important. Residents are encouraged to beautify their yards and may band together to clear an empty lot of debris or clean sidewalks.

With government assistance, neighborhood organizations may also improve local parks, develop better waste collection and cleaner streets, solve local parking problems, and possibly even landscape the neighborhood through tree planting and use of street furniture (Cassidy 1980: 125-239). Neighbors may become increasingly involved in local school activities and crime watch programs which provide greater surveillance of each others' property. Simultaneously, the neighborhood organization might monitor the deliberations of local zoning and planning boards to forestall any proposed development which might lead to the neighborhood's deterioration or gentrification (Weiler 1980). Social activities are always important components of the process of creating more cohesive neighborhoods. Block parties, ethnic festivals, picnics, and community suppers all reinforce the physical improvements with a greater commitment to the neighborhood.

Issues of Spatial Equity

Given its emphasis upon improvement of place, incumbent upgrading has important implications for social equity (Levy 1980: 303-4). By attacking redlining, for example, incumbent upgrading helps to remove a major inequity in investment policies. It equalizes investment and reinvestment across space and, thus, weakens the institutional mechanisms perpetuating the strong correspondence between socioeconomic position and environmental quality. A consequence of success, however, is that keeping existing residents in place makes it difficult for new households to join the neighborhood. The present residents do not move into better neighborhoods, leaving openings for those lower in socioeconomic status to occupy. Successful incumbent upgrading may, in fact, exacerbate socioeconomic, racial, and ethnic residential segregation (Albrandt and Cunningham 1979). Thus social equity may not be advanced.

From the viewpoint of social justice, incumbent upgrading must be considered a moderate strategy. It is not directed at the worst neighborhoods and their residents. Within most cities, some neighborhoods are gentrified, some undergo this process of upgrading, and many others (some in desperate need of assistance) are ignored. Thus, no victims of incumbent upgrading are visible but opportunities are lost. Both government and private funds are channeled to these and gentrifying neighborhoods and away from residential areas considered too deteriorated to be worth the effort. Incumbent upgrading does prevent some neighborhoods from falling into abandonment. To that extent, it may forestall any further increase in spatial inequity.

Theories of Neighborhood Succession

Traditional theories of neighborhood succession, based originally on the writings of the Chicago School of urban ecology (Park, Burgess and McKenzie 1925: 47-62) and later refined by empirical work in New York City (Hoover and Vernon 1962) and elsewhere, suggest that neighborhoods near the city center experience a succession of occupancy. They begin as middle- and upper-income areas. As the city grows, and middle-income groups move outward, the inner city neighborhoods age and deteriorate and are subsequently invaded by working-class, minority, and low-income people. Ultimately, they may be abandoned, converted to non-residential uses, or upgraded as houses with either public or private investment. However, urban theorists have seen this last possibility — residential renovation in the private sector — as neither inevitable nor likely (Gist and Fava 1964: 174). Urban neighborhoods thus generally pass through a series of stages: health, incipient decline, accelerated decline and abandonment (Albrandt and Brophy 1975:5-11; Cohen 1979; Gale 1980; Levy 1980).

Theoretical explanations for the increasingly frequent revival of decaying and sometimes abandoned residential neighborhoods are poorly developed. Most focus on a combination of changing demography and consumer tastes, rising housing and energy costs, and an emerging pro-urban ideology (London 1980: 83-88). Neil Smith (1979b), however, contended that such neo-classical explanations based on consumer demand are inadequate. They cannot explain which of many possible urban neighborhoods will be renewed or the roles that government and finance capital play in manipulating the process. Using evidence from Philadelphia, Smith argued that public and private interest groups knowingly, if not deliberately, implemented policies which promoted urban neglect and decline until land and other prices were sufficiently low for them to realize large profits through redevelopment. Government heavily subsidized corporate and household reinvestment (for example, UDAG) in gentrifying neighborhoods through tax benefits, historic preservation grants, and capital improvements. Gentrification as a process of neighborhood succession is diametrically opposed to the once-dominant theories of neighborhood change.

At the same time, certain policymakers and urban theorists propose to force reality into conformity with traditional theory. Whether under the rubric of triage (Baer 1976; Cassidy 1980: 285-7) or planned shrinkage (Starr 1978), they propose to direct public resources away from neighborhoods whose decline has accelerated or those already in a stage of abandonment. They propose a policy whereby services will be withdrawn from the worst neighborhoods, while the best neighborhoods receive normal public services. Governmental assistance will go mainly to those neighborhoods which can most easily be revitalized. This means that while neighborhoods undergoing gentrification and incumbent upgrading would continue to be helped, those neighborhoods and residents most in need of a major infusion of governmental assistance will be ignored. Such a policy can only increase inequity in residential revitalization.

6

Image, Sentiment, and the Revitalizing City

Urban revitalization changes not only the physical form of the urban environment but also transforms the image of the city, the ways in which it is perceived and experienced, and the psychological and emotional relationships between humans and urban places. Perceptual and experiential aspects are recognized as important by geographers and planners for whom purely economic or positivistic models of human behavior are inadequate (Gregory 1980).

As early as 1945, Walter Firey examined the endurance of Beacon Hill as an upper-class residential neighborhood able to resist encroachment from both the adjacent low-rent tenements of the West End and the contiguous central business district. He attributed its persistence to the sentiments which Bostonians, especially residents, had for Beacon Hill and its symbolic value. Since then, others have investigated feelings and attitudes such as attachment to, or fear of, places (Tuan 1974, 1979), reverence towards 'sacred spaces' (Graber 1976), and other variations in the ways a particular environment is perceived and comprehended (Holcomb 1972; Saarinen 1976). These perceptions affect human decisions and behavior which shape both landscape and human-environment relations (Buttimer and Seamon 1980; Canter 1977; Pocock and Hudson 1978; Porteous 1977; Relph 1976).

Revitalization efforts consciously try to remold the image of the city, to replace the perception of the city as a place of disinvestment, deterioration, crime, and poverty. "Psychology is a large part of the battle to keep cities alive" (Goldberger 1981: A18). The new image is to be one of progress, growth, vitality, and prosperity. Megastructures — huge, multi-purpose buildings — are important symbols conveying this new image, but they radically change the relationship of people to place. Another key dimension of revitalization, as seen from a phenomenological perspective, focuses on recapturing and reusing images of the past. Forms of historic preservation, adaptive reuse, and reconstruction of formerly bustling waterfront areas and 'Main Streets' link an ostensibly glorious past with a much-desired vibrant future. Modifying the environment to create these images produces qualitatively different human-environment relationships and severs emotional ties to place. A geography of urban revitalization would be incomplete without an exploration of these changes.

Creating a New Image

Revitalization requires an image of the reborn city (Redstone 1976: xvi; Appleyard 1979). Probably the most important impression is that of growth (or regrowth) and progress. Proponents of revitalization hope to replace the perception of decline with one of a healthy and expanding economy. Molotch (1976) argues that the contemporary American city can be viewed as a 'growth machine' in which localities vie for investments among themselves in order to stimulate development. New construction conveys an image of progress, and with it comes new opportunities for investment and consumption. Left unsaid is that growth also brings increased air and water pollution, traffic congestion, noise, and other problems, which are not borne equitably by all urban residents. The image of the vigorous, renascent city is carefully nurtured as the seed of the future material city.

To attract new investment and middle-class residents and consumers, the renovated image must have elements of solidity and security. It must inspire confidence that capital and labor invested in revitalization will be safe and profitable. An ideal image incorporates a physical symbol of the new city which will emphasize it on the cognitive maps of potential investors and residents. Recognition of the value of an Eiffel Tower or Empire State Building has led other cities to commission such symbols. St. Louis held a competition won by Eero Saarinen's Gateway Arch; Seattle built a Space Needle; and Houston, the Astrodome. Melbourne, Australia, went so far as to offer a $100,000 prize for the best idea for an image-making, "famous around the world" landmark to compete with Sydney's Opera House (Huxtable 1979). Boston's City Hall and the renovated Faneuil Hall, Detroit's Renaissance Center, Baltimore's Harborplace, or Atlanta's Peachtree Center are visual symbols and centerpieces of these cities' proclaimed rebirth.

Impressions of returning vitality require more than physical forms. The spirit becomes manifest in such activities as street festivals, beautification campaigns, cultural events, such as concert series and gallery exhibitions, winning sports teams, and even movies and publicity campaigns which tout the rebirth of the city. Thus New Brunswick, New Jersey, celebrates its economic recovery with a riverfront festival. Pittsburgh became the 'City of Champions' in the Seventies as the Steelers (football) won four Superbowls and the Pirates (baseball) won two World Series. Maynard Jackson, then major of Atlanta, declared that appropriations for the arts are excellent investments in a city's future (Jackson 1978: iii).

A recent study of the role of the arts in urban economic development, however, found that while investment in the arts can increase tourism to a limited extent, its main effect is to improve perceived quality of life. Quality of life has increasing importance in the locational decisions of firms and households, especially firms employing highly trained and mobile personnel whose middle-class lifestyle requires access to, if not utilization of, cultural facilities (Cwi 1980). Arts projects range in scale from refurbishing a theater, such as the Art Deco Astor Theater in Reading, Pennsylvania, or the renovation of a 1913 Symphony Hall in Springfield, Illinois, to the proposed $15 million San Antonio Performing Arts District which would include two renovated theaters, three cinemas, rehearsal studios, costume shops, and television and film production facilities. Occasions and facilities for entertainment, recreation, and culture all attract visitors to the city, provide employment, and, perhaps most importantly, improve the image of the city.

The Built Environment of Revitalization

As a new image of the city emerges, so also the material environment is reconstructed, creating a new experiential milieu. Central businss district revitalization often involves new construction, but renovation, adaptive reuse, or historical reconstruction of architecturally interesting residential, industrial, and commercial buildings is an increasingly popular strategy. Waterfronts and old main streets receive particular attention in the hope of regenerating their former vigor and ambiance.

Megastructures

A striking aspect of contemporary redevelopment is the large scale of the new CBD structures. In various cities 'megastructures,' or groups of skyscrapers, consolidate multiple functions into a few blocks. Clusters of high-rise buildings sprout on Bunker Hill in Los Angeles, where the thirty-five-story glass towers of the Bonaventure Hotel gleam in the sun. At ground level, the Bonaventure turns inward presenting an impenetrable two-story high defensive facade to the sidewalk pedestrian. The same architectural firm responsible for the Bonaventure also designed the $365 million Renaissance Center in Detroit, consisting of three massive towers on a multi-story windowless base. Renaissance Center, in fact, has been touted as the most expensive real estate development in history (Figure 5, p. 31). The name itself was chosen to signify Detroit's emergence from a dark age (Williams 1977: 6). Henry Ford wanted a visible symbol of the reversal of the city's fortunes, and Robert McCabe, president of Renaissance City, wanted it to be large:

> We wanted a brick-and-mortar operation that would start important physical things happening . . . We wanted to build something with the kind of critical mass that would make people say, Something's really happening in Detroit (quoted by Williams 1977:9).

Similar megastructures have been built in revitalizing and booming cities: the IDS Center in Minneapolis, Atlanta's Peachtree Center, New York's Citicorp Center, Place Bonaventure in Montreal, and the Greenway Plaza in Houston.

The megastructure contains a 'total environment' which is essentially self-contained. Suburbanites have safe and easy access by car to on-site, underground parking. From there, elevators go to air-conditioned upper levels providing a wide range of consumer goods and services. Exposure to the city and its perceived hazards can be avoided. Although they have been critically dubbed 'urban dinosaurs' and a 'Noah's Ark for the white middle class' (Conway 1977; Williams 1977), perhaps a more apt metaphor for such megastructures is 'white elephant.' (The kings of Siam would present enemy countries with white elephants which were relatively useless except for prestige, but which required heavy investment of resources for their maintenance.) Megastructures necessitate expensive public infrastructure (new access roads, sewers, street lighting, and security) and are frequently granted tax abatements (Hartman and Kessler 1978). After construction, they provide employment and services mainly for middle-class suburban commuters rather than for local city residents.

Megastructures alter both the vertical and horizontal scale of the built environment. In the vertical dimension they serve to redefine the skyline of the city, presenting a new profile which represents a dense concentration of capital investment and human activity (Figure 9). The skyline represents the city, just as the shopping mall surrounded

FIGURE 9   TRANSFORMATIONS IN THE SAN FRANCISCO SKYLINE (from Chester Hartman, *Yerba Buena, Land Grab and Community Resistance in San Francisco.* Published by New Glide Publications, 330 Ellis Street, San Francisco, CA 94102)

by acres of parking lots and the tract development represents suburbia. As one Los Angeles councilman commented: "We want to make Los Angeles look like a city. We need a skyline" (Hollie 1980). Thus, the corporate office building and the luxury high-rise replace the civic structures and cathedrals of earlier periods as symbols or urban place. They may serve a primordial need for perception of a cosmic scale vastly greater than the human (P. Smith 1973); they also represent the dominance of the secular, materialistic order.

Typically, the process of redevelopment, whether in the form of megastructures or simply contiguous buildings, also results in the consolidation of land holdings and in ownership of valuable central-city land by fewer investors. A few developers or investors take over blocks originally containing small businesses, residential buildings, and vacant lots owned by numerous small entrepreneurs (Figures 10 and 11). In Houston, for example, one corporation has purchased thirty-three blocks in the downtown and now owns twenty-five percent of the central city. Corporate and institutional imperialism is not new, having antecedents in the urban renewal programs of the past. It has been documented by Worthy (1976), Hartman (1974), and the UCLA Working Group of the Socialist Geographers' Speciality Group (1981). Aside from its material and political implications, such horizontal consolidation also results in increased density of development and fewer opportunities for diverse enterprises to locate in an area now dedicated solely to serving the middle class. Sharp boundaries appear between this development and the remaining zone of transition. At the same time, centralization of control conveys an image of risk-free investment, security, progress, and vitality.

Historic Preservation and Reconstruction

Revitalization efforts in many cities include the preservation and reconstruction of buildings and places which symbolize the city's past. This attempt to recapture history has several motives. In a time of diminishing natural resources, expensive credit, and high energy costs, renovation can be an economical way to provide attractive residential or commercial spaces. But there are more subjective, and perhaps equally important, motives for preserving old buildings and reconstructing facsimiles of past environments. They include a longing for an imagined or real halcyon past, aesthetic preference for historical architecture, attachment to the character of a place, and even patriotism and loyalty. The recent upsurge in America's interest in its past, spurred by the U.S. Bicentennial and the search for ethnic and racial roots, has made nostalgia a growth industry.

Cities represent massive concentrations of labor, material, and financial capital. Historical preservation is an effective technique for recovering the value of past investments (Chapman 1976:9). From the public perspective, the modernization and upgrading of public infrastructure and the renovation of existing buildings spares the cost of duplicating utilities and services in undeveloped fringe areas. From the private property owners' perspective, various tax incentives and government grants can hold down costs and provide tax write-offs for invested capital. Renovation reuses natural resources like brownstone and timber and requires less energy than construction of new buildings. Rehabilitation is more labor and less capital intensive than new construction, and thus creates more jobs for the same amount of investment. While some preservation jobs are highly skilled (the decorative stone cutter or wrought iron worker), the rehabilitation of old homes in historic neighborhoods provides training and employment in semi-skilled construction trades.

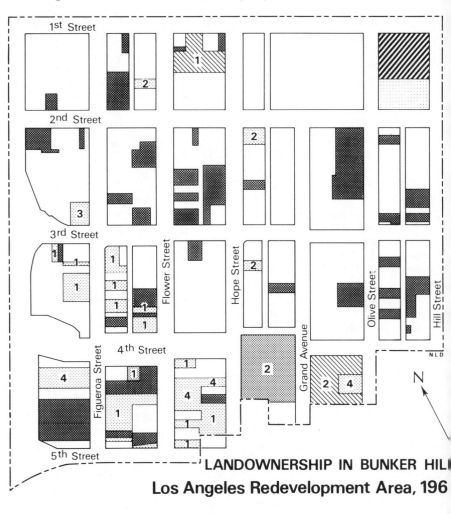

LANDOWNERSHIP IN BUNKER HILL
Los Angeles Redevelopment Area, 196

INDIVIDUAL OWNERS OF MULTIPLE PARCELS

BANKS & INSURANCE COMPANIES
1   Lincoln Savings
2   Pacific Mutual Life

PROPERTY MANAGEMENT & INVESTMENT CO
1   Greater Los Angeles Plan, Inc.
2   Bunker Hill Improvement Co.
3   Olympic Station, Inc.
4   Pery Co.

OTHER CORPORATIONS

PUBLIC UTILITIES
1   Southern California Edison
2   Pacific Telephone

PUBLIC LANDS

INDIVIDUALLY OWNED SINGLE PARCELS

FIGURE 10   OWNERSHIP OF BUNKER HILL, 1961 (compiled by the UCLA Working Group of the Socialist Geographers' Specialty Group, reproduced by permission)

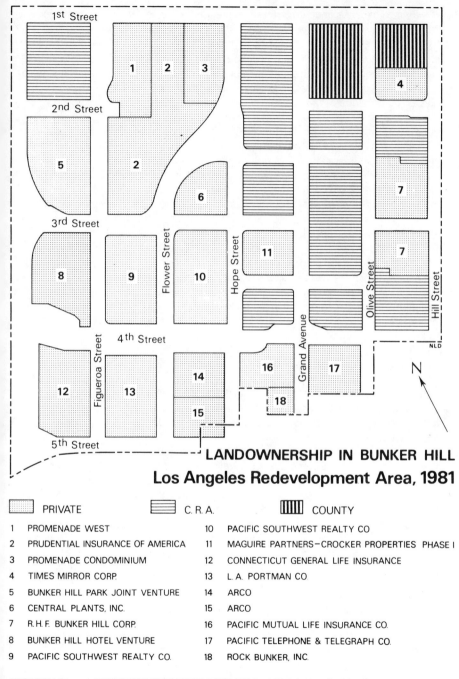

LANDOWNERSHIP IN BUNKER HILL
Los Angeles Redevelopment Area, 1981

PRIVATE   C. R. A.   COUNTY

1	PROMENADE WEST	10	PACIFIC SOUTHWEST REALTY CO
2	PRUDENTIAL INSURANCE OF AMERICA	11	MAGUIRE PARTNERS–CROCKER PROPERTIES PHASE I
3	PROMENADE CONDOMINIUM	12	CONNECTICUT GENERAL LIFE INSURANCE
4	TIMES MIRROR CORP.	13	L. A. PORTMAN CO
5	BUNKER HILL PARK JOINT VENTURE	14	ARCO
6	CENTRAL PLANTS, INC.	15	ARCO
7	R. H. F. BUNKER HILL CORP.	16	PACIFIC MUTUAL LIFE INSURANCE CO.
8	BUNKER HILL HOTEL VENTURE	17	PACIFIC TELEPHONE & TELEGRAPH CO.
9	PACIFIC SOUTHWEST REALTY CO.	18	ROCK BUNKER, INC.

FIGURE 11 OWNERSHIP OF BUNKER HILL, 1981 (compiled by the UCLA Working Group of the Socialist Geographers' Specialty Group, reproduced by permission). C.R.A., Community Redevelopment Agency.

Government has encouraged historic preservation by a variety of means. Federal, state, and some city governments have established registers of historic buildings and districts to protect significant buildings from demolition, control the quality and authenticity of restoration work, and discourage speculation. Guidelines and regulations in historically designated districts can restrict the sizes, architectural styles, construction materials, and uses of renovated and new buildings. Historic designation is sometimes resisted by developers who see it as an infringement of free enterprise and a barrier to large scale redevelopment. It can increase the cost of rehabilitating a building and thereby limit profits. On the other hand, district designation helps the business community by assuring investors that a tasteful and authentic restoration at one site will not lose value due to a tasteless and architecturally adulterated development nearby (Chapman 1976: 10). Moreover, the historic appeal of a building or district can often be capitalized as part of the sale price.

Numerous government programs have been used to finance historic preservation. The include direct grants and low interest loans for rehabilitation, publicly funded construction workers, tax write-offs of rehabilitation costs, National Endowment for the Arts planning studies, technical assistance by the Historic American Buildings Survey, and tax increment financing. Here the additional taxes generated by renovation are used solely within the historic district for additional improvements.

While important economic reasons exist for choosing preservation and renovation over demolition and reconstruction, other, less tangible motives shape the preservation movement. American cities are young by world standards. Until recently, the cultural and economic predilections for efficiency and modernity were clearly dominant. But over the last few years there has been a heightened appreciation for the value of preserving antiquated patches of the urban fabric. "A country without a past has the emptiness of a barren continent, and a city without old buildings is like a man without a memory" (Shankland, quoted in Uhlman 1976: 7). Restored buildings, monuments, parks, and neighborhoods can provide that societal memory of times past, times when the city flourished and its people prospered. Contrast, however, this image with the reality we described earlier (Chapter 2).

Historic preservation also maintains heterogeneity in urban form, a counterpoint to the glass and steel towers of modern central business districts and to the monotony of suburban residential developments. Old buildings add variety in architectural style, building materials and scale. More importantly, they can epitomize the spirit of a place and function as the key to its unique image. Peirce Lewis (1975b) has advocated historic preservation as a way of recapturing the *genius loci* dispersed by suburban decentralization and the multinucleated city. Decrying, as have others, the vacuum left by an earlier phase of urban renewal, Lewis (1975b:36) ridicules the notion that the symbolic functions of the CBD have been taken over by the suburban mall:

> *It is a rewarding exercise to imagine Lorenzo de' Medici ruling Florence from an air-conditioned palace at the intersection of two autostradas. Or reflect, if you please, on the spectacle of Socrates discoursing on excellence at the entrance of a shopping-center parking lot, with Muzak playing in the background."*

Lewis points out the recency of Americans' interest in the past, their new-found understanding of history as ". . . a dimension of human experience instead of a neat sanitary place with definite limits, cordoned off from the real world by white picket fences" (Lewis 1975b:37). This surge of enthusiasm for history has led to preservation activities especially in neighborhoods close to the central business district: Philadelphia's Society Hill, Benefit Street in Providence, and the Vieux Carré of New Orleans.

Not only architecture is conserved by historic preservation, but also the essence of place (Ford 1974). Place is what differentiates space and gives it meaning. "A place is a locus which is distinguished from the rest of the environment by the feelings held towards it" (Owen 1980: 9). One way to attach feelings to space and create a sense of place is through building. Geographers have noted that as part of the cultural landscape, the built environment represents a human memory bank. Environments contain a multitude of histories (Wagner 1972:3), representing one record of human experience. Architecture crystallizes consciousness of place, distinguishing it from undifferentiated space (Tuan 1977:107). Relph (1976) and Canter (1977), among others, have emphasized the psychological importance of a sense of place. Relph (1976:63) quoted Ian Nairn: "It seems a commonplace that almost everyone is born with the need for identification with his surroundings and a relationship to them — with the need to be in a recognizable place," and Harvey Cox: "the sense of continuity of place is necessary to people's sense of reality."

Historic preservation can rescue cities from the placelessness of contemporary international architecture. Cities around the world are becoming increasingly uniform. Both skyscrapers and the "signature" franchise architecture of Howard Johnson's, McDonalds, and Holiday Inn are ubiquitous (Rubin 1979). Consequently, cities have preserved part of their unique past as a way of recreating a distinct place and image. In many cities, little is left to preserve. Urban renewal, freeway construction and office towers have already replaced the pre-existing core. But in the zone of transition may be mills, warehouses, factories, and docks, which are newly perceived to have potential for redevelopment. Thus, the old industrial buildings of San Francisco's Jackson and Ghirardelli Squares have been renovated for office and retail space (Ford 1974). In Paterson, New Jersey, old mills and raceways designed by Pierre L'Enfant and Alexander Hamilton are being converted to artists' studios and apartments. Other "gritty cities" have embarked on similar projects, hoping that the conversion of old industrial buildings to new 'post-industrial' uses will recapture the city's vitality and simultaneously preserve its character (Proctor and Matuszeski 1978; Fleming 1981).

Preservation of historic places, nevertheless, is not a panacea, and has its critics. By necessity and choice, historic preservation is highly selective. Age is not enough. Buildings must look antique but not decayed (Lowenthal 1979: 108). Conscious preservation (as opposed to simple endurance) has often produced sanitized environments which appear ersatz even when authentic. Preservation reconstructs history, but sometimes it creates an imaginary and more acceptable past. We exclude less acceptable components of past environments (such as odors or the eclectic mixture of vernacular architecture) in favor of those aspects of the past which are fashionable today (Georgian brick, stained-glass windows). The selection, regrouping, and marking of buildings for historic preservation can produce a homogeneity of building age which never previously existed. On the other hand, most urban historic preservation also encourages artificial history — the 'Creole Disneyland' of the Vieux Carré where, "if the seedy old buildings are not picturesque enough, they can be made so by a generous frosting of cast-iron railings, made, if necessary, of genuine plastic" (Lewis 1975b:40).

Historic preservation is in demand by investors and consumers. The past is now profitable; history can be capitalized and sold. Whether for fear of the future, a crisis in social confidence, or simply a nostalgia for supposedly simpler times, Victoriana, Art

FIGURE 12   SOUTH STREET SEAPORT, NEW YORK, 1878
(engraving from *Harper's Weekly,* April 20, 1878, p. 316, provided
courtesy of Cobble Hill Cards, Southampton, New York)

Deco and other historical kitsch compete well with 'high tech' in popular taste. The recreated 'Old Main Street' at Disneyworld attracts more tourists than any genuine main street.

The Waterfront and Main Street

Seventy percent of United States' cities over 50,000 are located on a river, lake, or ocean. Many investors recognize the image-creating potential of redeveloped waterfront sites (Heritage Conservation and Recreation Service 1980:1). Piers, docks, and warehouses have lain moribund and decaying for decades, as railroads and tanker terminals took over their functions. But their proximity to the central business district, their structurally sound and aesthetically pleasing buildings, and a pervasive human attraction to water have led to rediscovery by developers, investors, and urban pioneers (Waterstone and Holcomb 1981).

By 1980, at least fifty cities had completed waterfront projects and another fifty had projects planned or underway (Heritage Conservation and Recreation Service 1980). They range from small parks such as three-quarter acre Grand Street Park in Brooklyn and thirty-acre Willamette Park in Portland, Oregon, to large multi-use developments in Boston around Quincy and Faneuil Hall Markets, Baltimore's Harborplace, Toledo's expansion of Owens-Illinois and Toledo Trust with the development of Promenade

Park, Seattle's Waterfront Park and Aquarium, and New York's South Street Seaport (Figures 12 and 13). In analyzing the factors which facilitate the success of a waterfront revitalization program, the Heritage Conservation and Recreation Service (1980:7) recommended that the first project should be widely used and easily accessible, and that it should be visible on a daily basis to as many people as possible. They suggest an amphitheater, ship restoration, or waterfront events.

Success breeds imitation. Quincy Market has been highly successful, both aesthetically and financially. The old market and warehouses have been converted into flourishing cafes, boutiques, and apartments. During 1980 the waterfront attracted a million visitors per week. Harborplace in Baltimore was designed by the same architect and built by the same developer as Quincy Market. In its first year of operation (1980-81), Harborplace attracted more visitors than Disneyland and created 2,300 jobs

FIGURE 13 ARTIST'S CONCEPTION OF THE SOUTH STREET SEAPORT AFTER REDEVELOPMENT (courtesy of The Rouse Company)

(Demarest 1981). In Baltimore, however, the market pavilions are new buildings rather than conversions, but appear to be equally attractive to tourists and shoppers. The same developer has proposed a similar design for the South Street Seaport in New York. However, environmental designers express growing concern about the uniformity of these projects. They fear that the 'exposed brick-spider plant syndrome' which pervades historic preservation will make revitalized waterfronts indistinguishable from each other.

These waterfront developments are highly successful commercially, but certainly do not recreate the historical quality of earlier waterfronts. Harborplace, Penn's Landing in Philadelphia, Quincy Market, and the future South Street Seaport are places for tourists, for office workers to eat lunch, and for conventioneers, not for sailors, dock workers, or the neighborhood vendors and customers who frequented these areas a century or two ago. Architectural critic Paul Goldberger (1981: A18) wrote of Harborplace:

> There is a sense that the environment is controlled, very controlled. This,
> in the end, is the real problem with places such as this. Harborplace
> takes conventional aspects of the urban experience, the little cafes and
> the energetic markets overflowing with produce, and turns them into
> something tame. It makes them easier than they are in the real world,
> more contained, more measured. Harborplace asserts that it is about
> spontaneity and variety, as real cities are; it is, in fact, about order and
> conformity.

Similar criticisms have been levelled against another common revitalization strategy — the conversion of the former commercial spine of the city into an up-to-date pedestrian mall. Pedestrian malls have been tried with varying success in many cities in the last twenty years. Hopefully, they would bring back some of the Main Street activity and vitality which gave the city an identity and a sense of place (Rifkind 1977:xi-xii).

Today, that street, once lined by a variety of utilitarian stores, is being "boutiqued." In revitalizing areas, small retail shops selling candles, coffee beans, designer jeans, macramé, organic food, and houseplants proliferate. They have names like Rag-Time Boutique, The Moveable Feast, Heads and Tails, Windy City Kite Works, or The Copper Carrot. As Joseph Epstein (alias Aristides 1975: 533) wrote, "Boutique America is the new urban renewal." 'Boutique America' may have set out to counter the creeping uniformity in American life, offer goods and services on a smaller, human scale, and replace mass-produced goods with handcrafted ones, but one boutiqued street is indistinguishable from another. Boutiqued streets contribute to the trend of placelessness in American cities. Moreover, the ephemeral nature of boutiques, whose speciality goods are highly susceptible to economic fluctuations, means these streets face a lack of continuity. Thus, just as the proponents of revitalization turn to waterfronts and Main Streets to recapture a past glory and uniqueness, they also set in motion the forces which may prevent their success and which may ultimately generate a uniformity which obviates the sense of place.

Loss of Familiar Locations

A major cost of urban revitalization is that people often lose environments to which they have developed strong emotional attachments. This loss occurs both when residents are displaced from their homes by gentrification or redevelopment, and when familiar environments are radically altered by revitalization activities.

The psychological costs of forced relocation during an earlier stage of urban renewal have been documented by Hartman (1963, 1966), Fried (1963), and Gans (1959, 1962), all of whom studied the redevelopment of Boston's West End. The West End site was a crowded, mixed-use, low-income neighborhood, perceived by urban planners as a slum (Jacobs 1961:11), but regarded with unreserved attachment by over three-quarters of its inhabitants (Hartman 1963). In Fried's (1963) study of women who said they liked living there very much, 73 percent suffered extreme grief after displacement. The women exhibited symptoms similar to those associated with a death in the family; Fried attributed the grief to the loss of a habitat. Displaced West Enders even returned to the area after demolition to walk through the rubble of their former homes in search, one might surmise, of now-severed emotional attachments (Porteous 1977:290).

Contemporary urban revitalization is less oriented towards slum clearance than previously, but there is nevertheless considerable involuntary displacement. Elderly people are particularly vulnerable to the stress of involuntary relocation partly because of the span of time over which their attachments to place have developed and partly because adjusting to a new environment is even more difficult with impaired mobility, vision, and other senses (Myers 1978). LeGates and Hartman (1981:52) cite studies showing that the primary group displaced by condominium conversion in the District of Columbia was the elderly, thirty percent of the displacees in Seattle were over 61, and in Boston's South End there was a sixty-five percent decrease in the over-65 age group. A recent study comparing the physical and mental health of over four hundred elderly residents in two apartment buildings in Florida, one of which was being converted into condominiums, found that the responses of the elderly people in the building scheduled for conversion conveyed a heightened sense of futility, disenchantment, confusion, and despair compared to those in the non-converted building. The same residents also reported physical symptoms such as headaches, dizziness, high blood pressure, and insomnia (Volsky 1981:47).

During gentrification, people without children often replace families. Twenty-nine percent of displacees in a St. Paul neighborhood were children (Sands 1979). Residents estimated a total of six children living in Boston's Bay Village after gentrification (Pattison 1977). Relocated children lose a familiar home range and a set of friends. Frequently they must adapt to a new school. Minority people, particularly poor Blacks and Hispanics, suffer more than non-minorities when displaced. The range of alternative housing opportunities open to them is limited by discrimination. Displaced minority people often relocate in nearby minority neighborhoods, adding to the stress of crowded living conditions. The invasion of White historic preservationists into previously Black neighborhoods, such as Georgetown and parts of Philadelphia and Charleston, not only displaces Blacks but eradicates part of their history (Newsom 1971).

Little is written about the psychological costs of the destruction of an environment to which one had develped attachment. The existing literature suggests that the radical transformation of place brings a sense of loss even to those who remain (Morris 1974). While recognizing the stimulation that environmental transformation can provide, one may also recall the loss of identity and a sense of belonging when a place one has known for many years is changed, sometimes beyond recognition. Familiar landmarks have been removed. The stores and 'hang-outs' which shaped one's daily movement no longer exist. Those places of congregation at which friendships were developed and nurtured are no longer available. New paths and places must be created and infused with the sentiment that was attached to their predecessors.

Several geographers have written about the contrasting conceptions of neighborhood and community held by long-term residents and newcomers in a gentrifying area. Long-term residents of Queen Village in Philadelphia viewed it not just as a locale, but also as a home, a community, and the setting for a whole way of life entailing extensive communal use of outdoor space. Newcomers, on the other hand, valued Queen Village not so much for its past, but for its potential. It provides a temporary habitat in their upward social and professional migration (Levy and Cybriwsky 1980:144). The contrasting values, lifestyles, and consumption patterns of the two groups eventually led to conflict and resentment by those residents who managed to resist displacement. The changes were cataclysmic. One Black pastor stated that money was eating the neighborhood alive.

This scenario is being repeated in many cities as working class and ethnic neighborhoods are transformed into chic, trendy habitats. People displaced by revitalization, and those whose environmental attachments are severed, are, from the perspective of the proponents of revitalization, simply victims of progress. Their losses, even if given public recognition, are viewed as the price which must be paid for revitalization. While the government might intervene to compensate such victims for part of the economic costs of displacement, the psychic costs are less easily mitigated. Loss of place requires long-term adjustment; it may never be recaptured.

The Changing Urban Milieu

The symbolic and psychological dimensions of urban revitalization usually receive little emphasis. New images and perceptions enhance the security of investments and contribute to the consumption needs of the middle class. When the symbols of working-class people are obliterated, their attachment to place severed, and their psychological well-being threatened by rapid and massive transformations in the urban environment, their concerns are unlikely to become public issues. The 'seamy side' of growth and progress is seldom scrutinized.

The overwhelming thrust of urban revitalization, with the sole exception of incumbent upgrading, is towards a corporate and middle-class definition of space and place. A controlled, homogenized, and hygenic environment may replace the rich vernacular of an earlier period, the diversity created by numerous, small investors. Visits from one revitalized central business district, gentrified neighborhood, or recaptured waterfront to the next blur in the memory. In megastructures and enclosed malls, the classic ambience of a traditional downtown — overstimulation, confusion, noise, excitement, heterogeneity — is absent. In its place is a color-coordinated, stylistically uniform visual environment; air conditioning which reduces temperature and olfactory variation; and smooth carpets and plastic which standardize tactile stimulation. One is not buffeted by wind or rain; one's ears are protected by Muzak from unwanted sounds; and even undesirable human elements are invisible. What sells in San Francisco and Detroit is profitably replicated in Boston and Los Angeles.

Finally, image and symbolism share in the uneven spatial investment in the city and the uneven development of urban space. Corporate and middle-class symbols are articulated and highlighted; those of the working class, poor, and ethnic and racial groups are neglected, unless, of course, they meet the needs of the proponents of revitalization. The resultant landscape is increasingly peaked where 'high' culture and 'post-industrial' symbolism predominate. In the troughs are the dashed sentiments and psychological disruptions experienced by the victims of 'progress.'

7

Social Justice and Urban Revitalization

Discussion of the geographical aspects of the history, causes, processes, and consequences of urban revitalization is not independent of our understanding of American society. While we have strived to be thorough and objective, our explanations and interpretations are not detached from our values and political perspective. This is true for all commentators — and as it must be. We cannot fully isolate normative concerns from empirical analysis (Rein 1976; Rule 1978). Even though it may be possible to describe the events, components, and participants in the process of urban revitalization with minimal bias, once explanations are formulated and consequences and long-run implications interpreted, academic and political values influence the resultant statements (Buttimer 1974; Stoddard 1981).

Our academic viewpoints of the analysis of urban revitalization are grounded in geography and urban planning. In providing an overview, many fascinating aspects of urban change, such as interrelationships among political actors, and the capital flows and financial mechanisms which drive redevelopment, are not considered. These issues have been explored by scholars in a number of disciplines (Boast 1980; Castells 1976; Fainstein and Fainstein 1981; Harvey 1978; Mollenkopf 1978). Our foci have been changing spatial patterns of people and resources, creation of new urban environments, and human relationships within those environments.

In addition to our disciplinary perspectives, our moral philosophy influences the problems we select for analysis, the diagnoses we develop, and the solutions we propose. Gilbert White (1972:102), for example, wrote that he would not do research "unless it promises results that would advance the aims of the people affected and unless [he was] prepared to take all practicable steps to help translate the results into action." Obviously, values and material interests help determine both theory and practice (Beauregard 1980). Our presentation of urban revitalization is no exception to the impossibility of value-free analysis. Thus, our ideological position should be as explicit as our disciplinary perspective. Therefore, this final chapter is devoted to a consideration of our theoretical perspective and to our recommendations for improving urban revitalization in a way compatible with the values and interests which we, and many others, hold (Clavel et al. 1980; Peet 1977a).

We have two objectives in this chapter. The first is to discuss the theoretical perspective which underlies our description and analysis of urban revitalization (Castells 1975; Mellor 1975; Peet 1977b). Of major importance is the emphasis which we give to the issue of social justice. The second objective emerges from our critical stance on urban revitalizaton. We have criticized many aspects of contemporary revitalization efforts. It now behooves us to offer recommendations for policy changes and for political action which would reverse the process of exclusionary revitalization, a process antithetical to principles of social justice.

Exclusionary Revitalization

One characteristic which differentiates our approach from conventional urban theory is a focus upon social justice. Previous, particularly neo-classical, theories have eschewed normative considerations of the distribution of the costs and benefits of urban change. In contrast, many researchers now make such analysis a major concern (Beauregard 1979; Coates *et al.* 1977; Harvey 1973; D. Smith 1977). Instead of arguing that cities move along a path from growth to decay or that they cycle naturally from one to the other over time, we argue instead that the processes of urban change are almost entirely subject to human control and direction. Key actors, such as developers in the case of urban revitalization, spur investment and growth, or, by withdrawing investment, abet decline. More importantly, revitalization processes do not, in the long run, necessarily lead to a 'more perfect' society. The trickling-down of benefits from increased investment is more ideology than reality. A constant progression toward solving urban ills and creating an environment in which all needs are met does not exist, nor does an impetus towards greater social justice.

Some principles of social justice in the contemporary United States can be enumerated. Poverty would be eliminated and economic security would be provided to all; racial and gender discrimination would not exist; political and economic decision-making would be democratic; and workers would have jobs which enhanced their sense of self-worth and contributed to a better society. Our society should have no unemployment; environmental amenities should be equally accessible; and everyone should have the opportunity to live in decent and affordable housing. Obviously, such an 'ideal' society is not imminent. A realistic position for progressive theorists and practitioners is to support those conditions which enhance social justice, that is, which create progress towards a society with these characteristics. Moreover, it is important that the process occur in a way which minimizes human misery accompanying change (Moore 1973).

Social justice has a spatial component. Just as the goods and services of society are distributed inequitably among individuals and social groups, so, too, are they among places. Obviously, natural resources, such as coal or fertile soil, are unevenly distributed, as is population itself. Indeed, economic efficiency demands that certain societal resources such as factories or cities be concentrated in those places or regions which have greatest locational advantages. However, efficiency is only one, albeit vital, criterion for assessing the optimum spatial distribution of goods and services. Equally important is the criterion of social justice. Does the spatial distribution enhance or reduce equity? The socially just distribution (which is equitable, giving to each according to need — but not necessarily equal or even) takes into account spatial variations in need, in positive and negative externalities, and in the distribution of environmental difficulties which must be overcome to develop a socially just society (Broadbent 1979; Harvey 1973:107-8; Herbert and Smith 1979; Lineberry 1977; D. Smith 1979).

Urban revitalization changes both the social and spatial distribution of goods and resources, but it usually does not entail a redistribution which favors low-income people or their neighborhoods. Rather, it further concentrates resources in areas which are dominated by upper- and middle-class people and reinforces their control over these urban spaces. Meanwhile, the negative externalities of redevelopment are often borne disproportionately by low-income people and neighborhoods. Indeed, urban revitalization is an exclusionary process. Those who initiate and guide it concentrate the benefits for themselves and for their class. The working class and the poor are divorced from deliberations over the direction of redevelopment and are burdened with a great majority of the costs. Urban revitalization is also exclusionary in a spatial sense. Only certain parts of the city are revitalized, and these become the domain of the upper and middle classes. Other areas of the city are left to deteriorate. The result is continued uneven development (N. Smith 1981).

The Process of Exclusion

The process of urban revitalization is controlled by a small number of groups and organizations. In the case of CBD redevelopment, relatively few major developers, investors, and real estate organizations work with the local government to reconstruct the center city. Opportunities for wider, more democratic participation are rare. The only influence that can be wielded by displaced small businesses and lower-income households comes through political protest and legal action. Otherwise, they are at the mercy of investors and elected officials who view a rejuvenated CBD as the salvation of the city, as well as a major opportunity for profit. Urban revitalization has the tacit, if not active, support of the middle class. Neighborhood commercial revitalization, in contrast, is more socially just. Neighborhood merchants, local financial institutions, governmental agencies, and sometimes local citizens work together to improve the commercial area, and they usually do so with a minimum of displacement. Still, CBD redevelopment has the greater impact on the city and its residents, but is controlled by a powerful few.

In residential rehabilitation, a similar pattern can be discerned. Gentrification is brought about by the actions of local real estate agents, small developers, local financial institutions, and a host of middle-class households. The process is less monolithic than CBD redevelopment, but still excludes and displaces the working class and poor. In incumbent upgrading, on the other hand, participation is much more widespread. Citizen input is solicited; the built environment and social relations are disrupted less. However, gentrification is the dominant process in revitalizing cities. It is more disruptive and most weakens social and spatial justice.

Overall, the domination of CBD redevelopment and gentrification within the process of urban revitalization leads to our assessment of urban revitalization as exclusionary. Investors and middle-class groups are in command, while mechanisms for democratic participation— what few exist — are ignored by local elected officials. Many urban residents and businesses are deprived of political input and control over their environment.

Consequences of Exclusion

The consequences of urban revitalization are as exclusionary as the process which creates them. More of the land and property in the central business district is captured by large investors and developers, real estate interests, and corporations.

Services, recreational and entertainment activities, and expanded employment opportunities are designed for the middle class. Psychologically, the downtown becomes upper- and middle-class space, reserved for their use and enjoyment, while the poor are pushed into less attractive parts of the city.

The costs of CBD revitalization are borne primarily by small-business people and working class and poor residents. Small manufacturing firms, which hire poorly skilled individuals, are eliminated; commercial establishments catering to the elderly and the poor are displaced; and low- and moderate-income housing units are demolished to make way for office buildings and luxury high-rise apartments. At worst, the upper and middle classes must bear the noise, pollution, and congestion caused by all of this new construction. But they do not lose homes and businesses, and their lives proceed essentially unhindered by redevelopment.

Redevelopment of the central business district may draw consumers away from some neighborhood commercial districts within the city. Similarly, in gentrifying neighborhoods, existing businesses are replaced by establishments which served the new, affluent residents with more expensive and specialized goods and services. Upgraded working class neighborhoods retain a better correspondence between neighborhood businesses and residents' consumer demands.

Gentrification deprives the working class and the poor of their home neighborhoods and focuses investment on enhancing the lives of the middle class. Those who are displaced receive little or no compensation and frequently end up residing in even more inferior neighborhoods — and paying *higher* prices for housing. Incumbent upgrading, on the other hand, is much less exclusionary when viewed in terms of existing residents. However, by discouraging the mobility of households into such neighborhoods, incumbent upgrading has the consequence of hindering spatial mobility within the city, thus doing little to improve the lives of the poorest urban residents.

All forms of urban revitalization have had the overall consequence of exacerbating, at best not diminishing, uneven development within the city. The end result is a city with some new, high-quality commercial environments, a few rehabilitated commercial areas providing goods and services for the working class, and a number of marginally stable or deteriorating commercial districts. In a large city such as New York or Philadelphia, CBD redevelopment may only cover parts of the central business district; gentrified commercial districts are small in number; and even those commercial areas being upgraded by local merchants are a small proportion of the city's shopping areas. It is clear that urban commercial revitalization does not reduce the social and spatial disparities attendant to retail activities. Rather the extremes — the high quality commercial environments and the low quality ones — become more disparate while a few commercial districts in the middle range are undergoing incumbent upgrading.

A similar pattern is discernible with residential rehabilitation. The result is the exacerbation of the uneven distribution of necessities and amenities. High-quality housing stock in amenity-rich locations is created for upper- and middle-class households, a few working-class neighborhoods are stabilized, and the poor are pushed into increasingly inferior environments. Capital investment flows to gentrified neighborhoods or residential enclaves in the revitalized CBD. A trickle of capital is directed to incumbent upgrading. In the remaining neighborhoods, particularly those which are not stable, disinvestment is common.

Urban revitalization is not a movement towards greater social and spatial justice. It is a classic case of uneven development under capitalism in which the rich and the middle class are favored, certain segments of the working class are provided benefits, and the poor and the lower class are ignored, or worse, further oppressed.

Urban Change and Urban Revitalization

The inequities of urban revitalization are neither natural nor inevitable. Nor does urban revitalization represent an overall improvement of the urban environment, a movement toward a more highly 'developed' society. The built environment does not inexorably deteriorate, become abandoned, and then undergo rehabilitation. In other countries, for example, parts of some cities have been maintained in good condition for centuries. Within the United States, the deterioration of the urban fabric is related to redlining, disinvestment, abandonment, and numerous other private and public actions (FHA mortgage insurance, interstate highways) which attract investment and people to other locations.

Similarly, redevelopment is not inevitable. A common scenario is that deteriorated neighborhoods will simply be abandoned and left empty for years. When rehabilitation does take place, it is usually initiated and controlled by investors, developers, real estate interests, and financial institutions who, at that time and place, foresee the opportunity for profitable investments. Perhaps the process begins with the government creating conditions which will attract capital to the city through public investment in parks, slum clearance, and land preparation. Alternatively, middle-class people find themselves excluded financially from the detached, single-family housing in the suburbs and desire city living. In a less organized fashion than private investors and government, they undertake gentrification.

In each of these three ways, revitalization is consciously and socially determined. Even with gentrification, small developers, real estate speculators, and financial institutions formulate the necessary conditions and provide direction. Urban revitalization is purposeful. It is not the result of the independent decisions of a multitude of consumers. Powerful actors set in motion the urban political-economy. At the same time, the decisions of these individuals and organizations — even those of elected officials and individual households — are constrained within and guided by the underlying logic of that political-economy. Within the United States, the pursuit of profit dominates economic entities. Governments are channeled in directions which preserve their fiscal stability, maintain the support of influential groups, and minimize civil discontent. Individual households make choices about location based on access to employment, availability of affordable housing, and the strength or weakness of institutional discrimination. Urban revitalization has social direction, and the direction it takes is set in general terms by the political-economic context (Beauregard *forthcoming*).

While our approach differs from conventional urban theory in positing this control of urban change by key actors in the political-economy, we also reject the notion that this particular process of urban change results in a general improvement of living conditions for all. For example, gentrification does not instigate a filtering process by which better housing units are made available to all, while the most deteriorated are abandoned. The application of filtering theory to even conventional neighborhood succession has been challenged (Hunter 1979; Zeitz 1979). During gentrification, the conversion of tenements, brownstones, and row houses to suitable residences for the affluent usually entails a reduction in the number of people occupying a building. Large families are replaced by small households in the same or larger living space. The number of housing units is reduced rather than increased, as filtering theory requires.

Restructuring the urban economy to represent the service and administrative dominance of a 'post-industrial' society eliminates many manufacturing jobs once available to the poorly-skilled, and substitutes menial service jobs having few opportunities for advancement or for high wages. Governmental funds spent in the CBD and in gentrifying neighborhoods mean less monies for those neighborhoods not part of the revitalization scheme. Revitalization brings higher prices for goods and services, particularly housing, and higher taxes. The poor and the working class are least able to afford them.

Even an overall improvement in the city's economy does not necessarily improve the lot of the least-advantaged residents. The mechanisms which would create social justice out of 'growth' do not function without the active intervention of government and advocacy organizations. While urban change brings both happiness and misery, neither of these is progressively or equally shared among all people. Much urban revitalization, in fact, is regressive. Environmental, social, and economic resources created by the process of redevelopment are transferred to those higher in the social hierarchy.

Urban Policy and Political Action

Despite our harsh criticisms, we support the continued investment in, and renewal of, existing cities. It is the renewal process and the distribution of the consequences to which we take exception. Numerous opportunities exist for modifying both government policies and private decisions, as well as for undertaking political actions which will reverse the exclusionary nature of present redevelopment efforts.

Declining cities need to receive private investment and government programs to stem deterioration and revive them economically. A 1980 Presidential Commission (President's Commission for a National Agenda for the Eighties 1980:11-21, 71-86) argued that decline is inevitable and that governmental policy must simply accept this fact and adapt to the growth of Sunbelt cities and the decline of the older, industrial cities. To the contrary, government should intervene, for many reasons, to reverse decline and to preserve urban environments in distress.

Analysis of past migrations suggests that only a small proportion of the population of declining cities will leave voluntarily. The quality of life should not deteriorate for those who stay. Much decline, in fact, is the result of the pursuit of profit by a small number of investors and financiers. Through their investments and disinvestments they dictate where and how people will live. This concentration of power is unjust, a clear violation of democratic prerogatives and process. In addition, people who have grown up and worked in cities have a right to remain. Attachment to place deserves recognition, and social networks should not be destroyed. Moreover, cities contain an elaborate built environment and supporting infrastructure which may have many years of useful life. The cost of duplicating these buildings, roads, bridges, and sewage and water systems in other locations is too high; money could be put to better use. Finally, just because these cities have declined does not mean that they are no longer viable. Certainly, some functions have left or been severely curtailed. Disinvestment and investment as part of a dynamic urban environment can be carried out in a socially just fashion. For these reasons, urban redevelopment is necessary to counteract socially unjust investment decisions and to compensate people for socially necessary disinvestment. Equitable urban revitalization, however, requires the active support of governmental bodies and political action by working-class organizations. The contemporary procedures and consequences of revitalization are unacceptable.

In the early stages of urban decline, government must act more quickly to stem deterioration and compensate its victims. A major factor in decline is out-migration of capital and the subsequent closing of manufacturing and commercial establishments. Government must retain capital investment, maintain jobs for urban residents, and, thus, preserve (and even expand) the amount of wealth and income in the community. Simultaneously, it must assure a socially just distribution of these valued resources. The social and economic programs of the government should be used to smooth the transition of the economy from an industrial base to a high technology and administrative-service base. Disinvestment in certain economic activities is necessary as products become outmoded and other countries produce them more cheaply (Thurow 1980:76-102). Negative consequences can be avoided, however, by developing new employment opportunities, retraining those initially left unemployed, and maintaining incomes during the interim period.

In addition, the national government must develop greater control over the movement of firms and of plant closings (Bluestone *et al.* 1981). Often such migrations and closings result in greater profit for the firm but large costs for society. A national policy must be formulated which will eliminate disruptions which benefit firm owners but force working-class people to leave loved places and communities, and migrate to where investors have decided jobs should be developed. Such policies, supplemented by programs to redistribute income (tax policies) and upgrade the environment, would enable cities to avoid decline and thus eliminiate the need for large-scale revitalization efforts.

If revitalization is necessary, government should intervene, first, to make redevelopment procedures more democratic, and, second, to spread the benefits and costs of change across both space and social groups. Short of taking over urban revitalization from the private sector, government must begin by obtaining better control of its subsidies to developers. Mechanisms must be designed which will capture the profits made from redevelopment and redistribute them. The first requires that government be able to distinguish when assistance is necessary to attract investors and when such assistance is only a 'gift' to an investor who would have come into the city without it (Goodman 1979). Government must then direct some of the profits for use in other parts of the city. Major investors, developers, and real estate organizations involved in CBD redevelopment should be taxed not only on the basis of increases in property value, but also on the returns to their investments. Tax abatements, for example, should be repaid once the investment has proven successful. Residential and commercial gentrifiers should be taxed at higher rates in order to provide compensation to the victims of gentrification and to generate public funds for use in other parts of the city.

At the same time, government must devise mechanisms for providing greater social control over redevelopment. Private investors must not be allowed to ignore the needs of the working class within the city by arguing that the benefits of revitalization will accrue to the community as a whole. In return for the opportunity to invest, their plans should require approval by citizen advisory boards and should make necessary concessions to various groups and neighborhoods in order to obtain that approval. Of utmost importance is that this approach should apply to governmental programs and policies, as well as to private sector redevelopment activities.

To achieve equitable revitalization requires greater and more effective political activity on the part of working-class and low-income organizations. Neighborhood groups frequently arise to resist redevelopment. Often, however, these groups lack resources for long-term resistance, and become aware of the redevelopment process only after major decisions have been made and resources allocated (Stone 1976). In fact, political resistance to urban redevelopment is not as common in the Eighties as during the early Sixties when Urban Renewal was first underway. Much of the major demolition of neighborhoods has been accomplished and now it is the marginal districts containing the elderly, poor, minorities, and small businesses that are being revitalized. These groups are not likely to make themselves a major obstacle to the objectives of private investors and elected officials. Political action to resist gentrification and support incumbent upgrading is more common. Negative impacts of these revitalization activities are more apparent, and the groups affected less diffuse and more capable of organizing. Still, effective opposition is difficult, and gentrification once started usually overwhelms the neighborhood and its existing residents.

Despite this pessimistic assessment, working-class and low-income households have avenues of positive action open to them. They must begin by developing strong neighborhood and city-wide organizations concerned with issues of redevelopment, and then form coalitions with organizations which have related interests (labor unions or local social service agencies). Neighborhood-based organizations must then gain control over their local economy and over those forces which shape the built environment. One option is the formation of Community Development Corporations (CDC's) to establish businesses which will provide jobs, rehabilitate housing, and keep capital within the neighborhood (Harrison 1974:167-84). The 'profits' from such enterprises are reinvested in the community, and the decisons about investment are made by neighborhood advisory boards. Another option is to encourage greater public ownership of housing, commercial establishments, and local industries (Carnoy and Shearer 1980). Public ownership means ownership by local people, not the government, most likely in the form of cooperatives. The goal in both cases, CDC's and cooperatives, is to sever the problematic relationship between profit-making and the quality of life.

City-wide organizations must develop the capability of monitoring revitalization as it occurs throughout the city. This means anticipating the investments of developers, assuring that legal procedures are followed and governmental regulations imposed, and attesting that government protection and compensation are extended to those whose lives are disrupted. This knowledge, however, is only useful if it can be combined with political influence. Thus, city-wide organizations concerned with inclusionary revitalization must infiltrate local electoral politics and exploit all opportunities for involvement with bureaucratic decision-making. Coalitions of neighborhood groups can put redevelopment on the political agenda at both local and state government levels. Elected officials and local bureaucrats must understand that avoiding issues of social justice will result in public condemnation and possible loss of influence.

Obviously, these few comments on government policies and political action constitute only the beginnings of an analysis of the ways in which the present process of exclusionary, inequitable growth can be reversed. Urban growth, urban decline, and the processes which create these conditions are directed by major groups within society who wield the political and economic influence to achieve their interests. Their concern is not social justice. If social justice is to be achieved, and if urban revitalization is to be made a participatory process, urban residents must band together and pressure government and the private sector. Without such political activities, cities will remain uneven in development, and, as a society, we will come no closer to social justice.

Bibliography

Abravanel, M.D. and P.K. Mancini. 1980. "Attitudinal and Demographic Constraints," pp. 27-47 in Rosenthal (1980).

Albrandt, R.S. Jr. and P.C. Brophy. 1975. *Neighborhood Revitalization.* Lexington, MA: D.C. Heath.

Albrandt, R.S. Jr. and J.V. Cunningham. 1979. "The Ungreening of Neighborhood Planning," Vol. 4, pp. 6-22 in S. Hines *et al.* (1979).

Alcaly, R.E. and H. Bodian. 1977. "New York's Fiscal Crisis and the Economy," pp. 30-58 in Alcaly and Mermelstein (1977).

Alcaly, R.E. and D. Mermelstein (editors). 1977. *The Fiscal Crisis of American Cities.* New York: Vintage.

Allen, I. 1980. "The Ideology of Dense Neighborhood Redevelopment: Cultural Diversity and Transcendent Community Experience," *Urban Affairs Quarterly* 15, 4: 409-428.

Allman, T.D. 1978. "The Urban Crisis Leaves Town, and Moves to the Suburbs," *Harpers* 257, 1543: 41-56.

Alpern, D.M. 1979. "A City Revival?" *Newsweek* 97,3: 28-30, 33-35.

Altshuler, A. 1979. *The Urban Transportation System.* Cambridge, MA: The M.I.T. Press.

Altschuler, A. 1969. "The Potential of 'Trickle Down'," *The Public Interest* 15 (Spring): 46-56.

American Industrial Priorities Report. 1980. "A Tool With Many Handles," *American Industrial Priorities Report* 12,4: 26-27.

Anderson, M. 1964. *The Federal Bulldozer.* Cambridge, MA: The MIT Press.

Appleyard, D. 1979. "The Environment as a Social Symbol," *Journal of the American Planning Association* 45: 143-153.

Aristides. 1975. "Boutique America!" *American Scholar* 44,4: 533-539.

Ashton, P.J. 1978. "The Political Economy of Suburban Development," pp. 64-89 in Tabb and Sawers (1978).

Auger, D. 1979. "The Politics of Revitalization in Gentrifying Neighborhoods: The Case of Boston's South End," *Journal of the American Planning Association* 45: 515-522.

Baer, W.C. 1976. "On the Death of Cities," *The Public Interest* 45 (Fall): 3-19.

Beauregard, R.A. 1979. "Splicing Welfare Analysis and Human Geography," *Geographical Survey* 8,1: 33-35.

Beauregard, R.A. 1980. "Thinking About Practicing Planning," pp. 308-25 in Clavel *et al.* (1980).

Beauregard, R.A. forthcoming. "Structural Analysis and Urban Redevelopment," *Comparative Urban Research.*

Beauregard, R.A. and R. Cousins. 1981. "The Spatial Distribution of Revitalizing Cities in the United States," *Rutgers Geography Discussion Paper* No. 19. New Brunswick, NJ: Rutgers University, Department of Geography.

Beauregard, R.A. and B. Holcomb. 1979. "Dominant Enterprises and Acquiescent Communities: The Private Sector and Urban Revitalization," *Urbanism Past and Present* 8 (Summer): 18-31.

Bergman, E.F. 1978. "Gentrification in New York City," *Proceedings,* Middle States Division of the Association of American Geographers 12:12-15.

Birch, E.L. 1978. "Woman-Made America: The Case of Early Public Housing," *Journal of the American Institute of Planners* 44: 130-144.

Black, J.T. 1980. "Private Market Housing Renovation in Central Cities: An Urban Land Institute Survey," pp. 3-12 in Laska and Spain (1980).

Bluestone, B., B. Harrison, and L. Baker. 1981. *Corporate Flight.* Washington, DC: Progressive Alliance.

Blumenthal, S. 1979. "Skyscrapers and Ferns Create New Poor," *In These Times* 3,13: 19.

Boast, T. 1980. "Urban Resources, the American Capital Market, and Federal Programs," pp. 73-92 in D. Ashford (editor), *National Resources and Urban Policy.* New York: Methuen.

Brambilla, R., G. Longo, and V. Dzurinko. 1977. *American Urban Malls: A Compendium.* Washington, DC: Government Printing Office.

Broadbent, T.A. 1979. *Planning and Profit in the Urban Economy.* New York: Methuen.

Brozen, N. 1979. "For Some Suburban Families, City Living Has Become Alluring," *The New York Times* (February 20).

Bunce, H.L. and N.J. Glickman. 1980. "The Spatial Dimensions of the Community Development Block Grant Program: Targeting and Urban Impacts," pp. 515-541 in N.J. Glickman (editor), *The Urban Impacts of Federal Policies.* Baltimore, MD: The Johns Hopkins University Press.

Buttimer, A. 1974. *Values in Geography.* Washington, DC: Association of American Geographers, Commission on College Geography, *Resource Paper* 24.

Buttimer, A. and D. Seamon. 1980. *The Human Experience of Space and Place.* New York: St. Martin's.

Canter, D. 1977. *The Psychology of Place.* New York: St. Martin's.

Carnoy, M. and D. Shearer. 1980. *Economic Democracy.* Armonk, NY: M.E. Sharpe.

Cassidy, R. 1980. *Livable Cities.* New York: Holt, Rinehart and Winston.

Castells, M. 1975. "Urban Sociology and Urban Politics," *Comparative Urban Research* 3,1: 7-13.

Castells, M. 1976. "The Wild City," *Kapitalistate* 4-5 (Summer): 2-30.

Castells, M. 1977. *The Urban Question.* Cambridge, MA: The M.I.T. Press.

Chadwick, G.F. 1966. *The Park and the Town.* New York: Frederick A. Praeger.

Chapman, B. 1976. "The Growing Public Stake in Urban Conservation," pp. 9-13 in National Trust for Historic Preservation (1976).

Chernoff, M. 1980. "Social Displacement in a Renovating Neighborhood's Commercial District: Atlanta," pp. 204-219 in Laska and Spain (1980).

Cincin-Sain, B. 1980. "The Costs and Benefits of Neighborhood Revitalization," pp. 49-75 in Rosenthal (1980).

Clark, G.L. 1980. "Capitalism and Regional Inequality," *Annals,* Association of American Geographers 70: 226-237.

Clavel, P., J. Forester, and W.W. Goldsmith (editors). 1980. *Urban and Regional Planning in an Age of Austerity.* New York: Pergamon.

Clawson, M. 1975. "Factors Affecting Suburbanization in the Postwar Years," pp. 182-188 in Gale and Moore (1975).

Clay, P. 1979. *Neighborhood Renewal: Middle Class Resettlement and Incumbent Upgrading in American Neighborhoods.* Lexington, MA: D.C. Heath.

Clay, P. 1980. "The Rediscovery of City Neighborhoods: Reinvestment by Long-Time Residents and Newcomers," pp. 13-26 in Laska and Spain (1980).

Clement, A. 1981. "The Gallery II — Urban Development for Whom?" *The Organizer* 7,1: 12.

Coates, B.E., R.J. Johnston, and P.L. Knox. 1977. *Geography and Inequality.* New York: Oxford University Press.

Cohen, R. 1979. "Neighborhood Planning and Political Capacity," *Urban Affairs Quarterly* 14,3: 337-382.

Committee on Banking, Housing and Urban Affairs. 1973. *The Central City Problem and Urban Renewal Policy.* Washington, DC: Government Printing Office.

Congressional Budget Office. 1978. *Barriers to Urban Economic Development.* Washington, DC: Government Printing Office.

Conway, W.G. 1977. "The Case Against Urban Dinosaurs," *Saturday Review* 4 (May 14): 12-15.

Cox, K. (editor). 1978. *Urbanization and Conflict in Market Societies.* Chicago, IL: Maaroufa.

Cox, K. 1979. *Location and Public Problems.* New York: Methuen.

Cox, W.E. Jr. 1969. "A Commercial Structure Model for Depressed Neighborhoods," *Journal of Marketing* 33(July): 1-9.

Cranz, G. 1978. "Changing Role of Urban Parks," *Landscape* 22,3: 9-18.

Cwi, D. 1980. *The Role of the Arts in Urban Economic Development.* Washington, DC: U.S. Department of Commerce.

Cybriwsky, R.A. 1978. "Social Aspects of Neighborhood Change," *Annals,* Association of American Geographers 68: 17-33.

Cybriwsky, R.A. 1980. "Revitalization Trends in Downtown Area Neighborhoods," pp. 21-36 in S.D. Brunn and J.O. Wheeler (editors), *The American Metropolitan System: Present and Future.* New York: John Wiley and Sons.

Daniel, E.C. 1977. "Small Business Administration Beefs Up 502 Programs to Bring Help to Urban Commercial Areas," *Journal of Housing* 34,8: 392-393.

Davies, H.W.E. 1980. "Neighborhood Revitalization: The British Experience," pp. 255-278 in Rosenthal (1980).

Demarest, M. 1981. "He Digs Downtown," *Time* 118,8: 42-53.

Derthick, M. 1972. *New Towns In-Town.* Washington, DC: The Urban Institute.

DeVito, M.J. 1980. "Retailing Plays Key Role In Downtown Renaissance," *Journal of Housing* 37,4: 197-200.

Dingemans, D. 1979. "Redlining and Mortgage Lending in Sacramento." *Annals,* Association of American Geographers 69: 225-239.

Downs, A. 1979. "Key Relationships Between Urban Development and Neighborhood Change," *Journal of the American Planning Association* 45: 462-472.

Editorial Collective. 1978. "Uneven Regional Development: An Introduction to This Issue," *The Review of Radical Political Economics* 10,3: 1-12.

Fainstein, S.S. and N.I. Fainstein. 1974. *Urban Political Movements.* Englewood Cliffs, NJ: Prentice-Hall.

Fainstein, S.S. and N.I. Fainstein. 1976. "The Federally Inspired Fiscal Crisis," *Society* 13,4: 27-32.

Fainstein, S.S. and N.I. Fainstein. 1981. "Production and Welfare in American Cities." Paper presented at the conference on "New Perspectives on the Urban Political Economy," Washington, DC.

Firey, W. 1945. "Sentiment and Symbolism as Ecological Variables," *American Sociological Review* 10: 140-148.

Fleetwood, B. 1979. "The New Elite and an Urban Renaissance," *The New York Times Magazine* (January 14): 16-20, 22, 26, 34-35.

Fleming, R.L. 1981. "Recapturing History: A Plan for Gritty Cities," *Landscape* 25,1: 20-27.

Forbes, S. 1977. "How Does Neighborhood Commercial Revitalization Work in Economic Terms?" pp. 146-152 in Goldstein and Davis (1977).

Ford, L. 1974. "Historic Preservation and the Sense of Place," *Growth and Change* 5,2: 33-37.

Ford, L. 1976. "Historic Preservation and the Inner City: The Perception of German Village by Those Just Beyond," *Proceedings,* Association of American Geographers 8: 110-113.

Ford. L. and R. Fusch. 1978. "Neighbors View German Village," *Historic Preservation* 30 (July-September): 37-42.

Fossett, J.W. and R.P. Nathan. 1980. "The Prospects For Urban Revival." Princeton, NJ: Princeton University, unpublished document.

Fried, M. 1963. "Grieving for a Lost Home: Psychological Costs of Relocation," pp. 151-171 in L.J. Duhl (editor), *The Urban Condition.* New York: Basic Books.

Frieden, B.J. and M. Kaplan. 1975. *The Politics of Neglect.* Cambridge, MA: The M.I.T. Press.

Friedman, L. M. 1968. *Government and Slum Housing.* Chicago, IL: Rand McNally.

Fusch, R. 1980. "A Case of Too Many Actors?: Columbus," pp. 156-172 in Laska and Spain (1980).

Fusfeld, D.R. 1968. *The Basic Economics of the Urban and Racial Crisis.* Ann Arbor, MI: The Union for Radical Political Economics.

Gale, D.E. 1979. "Middle Class Resettlement in Older Urban Neighborhood: The Evidence and the Implications," *Journal of the American Planning Association* 45: 293-304.

Gale, D.E. 1980. "Neighborhood Resettlement: Washington, DC," pp. 95-115 in Laska and Spain (1980).

Gale, S. and E.G. Moore (editors). 1975. *The Manipulated City.* Chicago, IL: Maaroufa.

Gans, H.J. 1959. "The Human Implications of Slum Clearance and Relocation," *Journal of the American Institute of Planners* 25: 15-25.

Gans, H.J. 1962. *The Urban Villagers.* New York: The Free Press.

Gans, H.J. 1965. "The Failure of Urban Renewal," *Commentary,* 34,4: 29-37.

Gans, H.J. 1968. "Outdoor Recreation and Mental Health," pp. 108-125 in H.J. Gans, *People and Plans.* New York: Basic Books.

Gasser, W. 1979. "The Southeast Land Bank," *Journal of the American Planning Association* 45: 532-537.

Gelfand, M. 1975. *A Nation of Cities.* New York: Oxford University Press.

Ginzberg, E. and G.J. Vojta. 1981. "The Service Sector of the U.S. Economy," *Scientific American* 244,3: 48-55.

Gist, J.R. 1980. "Urban Development Action Grants: Design and Implementation," pp. 237-252 in Rosenthal (1980).

Gist, N.P. and S. Fava. 1964. *Urban Society.* New York: Crowell.

Goering, John M. 1979. "The National Neighborhood Movement: A Preliminary Analysis and Critique," *Journal of the American Planning Association* 45: 506-514.

Goldberger, P. 1981. "Baltimore Marketplace: An Urban Success," *The New York Times* (February 18).

Goldstein, B. 1977. "Neighborhood Commercial Revitalization: A Practitioner's Perspective," pp. 3-15 in Goldstein and Davis (1977).

Goldstein, B. and R. Davis (editors). 1977. *Neighborhoods in the Urban Economy.* Lexington, MA: D.C. Heath.

Goldstein, R. 1980. "The Gentry Comes to the East Village," *The Village Voice,* 25,20 (May 19): 18, 42.

Goodman, A.C. and R. Shain. 1980. *Displacement: A Selected Bibliography.* Monticello, IL: Vance Bibliographies.

Goodman, R. 1979. *The Last Entrepreneurs.* New York: Simon and Schuster.

Gordon, D.M. 1978. "Capitalist Development and the History of American Cities," pp. 25-63 in Tabb and Sawers (1978).

Gorham, W. and N. Glazer (editors). 1976. *The Urban Predicament.* Washington, DC: The Urban Institute.

Graber, L. 1976. *Wilderness as Sacred Space.* Washington, DC: Association of American Geographers.

Gregory, D. 1978. *Ideology, Science and Human Geography.* New York: St. Martin's.

Grier, G. and E. Grier. 1977. *Movers to the City: New Data on the Housing Market in Washington, D.C.* Washington, DC: Washington Center for Metropolitan Studies.

Grier, G. and E. Grier. 1978. *Urban Displacement: A Reconnaissance.* Washington, DC: U.S. Department of Housing and Urban Development.

Groton, T. 1979. "Detroit Reborn," *Planning* 45,7: 15-19.

Gruen, V. and L. Smith. 1960. *Shopping Towns USA: The Planning of Shopping Centers.* New York: Van Nostrand Reinhold.

Harrison, B. 1974. *Urban Economic Development.* Washington, DC: The Urban Institute.

Hartman, C. 1963. "Social Values and Housing Orientations," *Journal of Social Issues* 19: 113-131.

Hartman, C. 1966. "The Housing of Relocated Families," pp. 293-335 in J.Q. Wilson (editor), *Urban Renewal: The Record and the Controversy.* Cambridge, MA: The M.I.T. Press.

Hartman, C. 1974. *Yerba Buena: Land Grab and Community Resistance in San Francisco.* San Francisco, CA: Glide Publications.

Hartman, C. 1979a. "Displacement: A Not So New Problem," *Social Policy* 9,5: 22-27.

Hartman, C. 1979b. "Comment on 'Neighborhood Revitalization and Displacement: A Review of the Evidence,'" *Journal of the American Planning Association* 45: 488-491.

Hartman, C. and R. Kessler. 1978. "The Illusion and the Reality of Urban Renewal," pp. 153-178 in Tabb and Sawers (1978).

Harvey, D. 1973. *Social Justice and the City.* Baltimore, MD: The Johns Hopkins University Press.

Harvey, D. 1975. "The Political Economy of Urbanization in Advanced Capitalist Societies: The Case of the United States," pp. 119-163 in G. Gappert and H. Rose (editors), *The Social Economy of Cities.* Beverly Hills, CA: Sage.

Harvey, D. 1977. "The Geography of Capitalist Accumulation," pp. 263-292 in Peet (1977a).

Harvey, D. 1978. "On Countering the Marxian Myth-Chicago Style," *Comparative Urban Research* 6(2,3): 28-45.

Herbers, J. 1980a. "The Cities Call Out for Help But Their Voice Is Fainter," *The New York Times* (August 11).

Herbers, J. 1980b. "Study Says Old Cities Continue to Decline Despite Rejuvenation," *The New York Times* (July 7).

Herbert, D. and D.M. Smith. 1979. *Social Problems and The City.* Oxford, U.K.: Oxford University Press.

Heritage Conservation and Recreation Service. 1980. *Urban Waterfront Revitalization: The Role of Recreation and Heritage.* Washington, DC: U.S. Department of the Interior.

Hines, S.M. et al. (editors). 1979. *South Atlantic Urban Studies.* Charleston, SC: College of Carolina.

Hodge, D.C. 1980. "Inner City Revitalization as a Challenge to Diversity?: Seattle," pp. 187-203 in Laska and Spain (1980).

Holcomb, B. 1972. *The Influence of Culture on Perception of The Urban Environment.* Boulder, CO: University of Colorado, unpublished Ph.D. dissertation.

Holcomb. B. 1981. "Women's Roles in Distressing and Revitalizing Cities," *Transition* 11,2: 1-6.

Holcomb, B. and R.A. Beauregard. 1980a. "Spatial Targeting vs. Political Dispersion: Ramifications of Urban Development Action Grants," *Research in Contemporary and Applied Geography* 4,4: 65-83.

Holcomb, B. and R.A. Beauregard. 1980b. "The Impact of an Urban Program on Distressed States," paper presented at the Annual Meeting of the Middle States Division of the Association of American Geographers, Newark, Delaware.

Hollie, P. 1980. "Downtown Los Angeles Getting New Focus," *The New York Times* (November 4).

Hoover, E.M. and R. Vernon. 1962. *Anatomy of a Metropolis.* Garden City, NY: Doubleday.

Horsley, C. 1980. " 'Revitalization' Held to Be Spotty," *The New York Times* (June 1).

Hunter, A. 1979. "The Urban Neighborhood: Its Analytical and Social Contexts," *Urban Affairs Quarterly* 14,3: 267-288.

Huxtable, A.L. 1979. "Selling Cities Like Soap," *The New York Times* (January 16).

Jackson, M. 1978. "Introductory Letter," in U.S. Conference of Mayors, *The Taxpayers' Revolt and the Arts.* Washington, DC.

Jacobs, J. 1961. *The Death and Life of Great American Cities.* New York: Random House.

Jacobs, S.S. and E.A. Roistacher. 1980. "The Urban Impacts of HUD's Urban Development Action Grant Program, or Where's the Action in Action Grants?" pp. 335-362 in Norman J. Glickman (editor), *The Urban Impacts of Federal Policies.* Baltimore, MD: The Johns Hopkins University Press.

James, F.J. 1980. "The Revitalization of Older Urban Housing and Neighborhoods," pp. 130-160 in Arthur P. Solomon (editor), *The Prospective City.* Cambridge, MA: The M.I.T. Press.

Judd, D.R. 1979. *The Politics of American Cities.* Boston, MA: Little Brown and Company.

Keating, R. 1980a. "Columbia Devours the Upper West Side," *The Village Voice,* 25,20: 1,13-16.

Keating, R. 1980b. "The Next Neighborhood: Long Island City," *New York* 13,31: 20-25.

Keith N.S. 1973. *Politics and the Housing Crisis Since 1930.* New York: Universe Books.

Kotler, M. 1980. "Is Residential Displacement a Critical Urban Problem? — Pro," *Urban Concerns* 1,2: 31-40.

Kuttner, B. 1980. "Stone Soup: Why Neighborhood Housing Services Works," *Working Papers for A New Society* 7,4: 32-41.

Larmarche, F. 1976. "Property Development and the Economic Foundations of the Urban Question," pp. 85-118 in C.G. Pickvance (editor), *Urban Sociology.* New York: St. Martin's.

Laska, S.B. and D. Spain (editors). 1980. *Back to the City.* Elmsford, NY: Pergamon.

Laska, S.B. and D. Spain. 1979. "Urban Policy and Planning in the Wake of Gentrification," *Journal of the American Planning Association* 45: 523-531.

Lauria, M. 1980. *Community Controlled Redevelopment: South Minneapolis.* Minneapolis, MN: University of Minnesota, unpublished Ph.D. dissertation.

Leavitt, H. 1970. *Superhighway-Superhoax.* New York: Doubleday.

LeGates, R. and C. Hartman. 1981. *Displacement.* Berkeley, CA: National Housing Law Project, Legal Services Anti-Displacement Project.

Levatino, A.M. 1978. *Neighborhood Commercial Rehabilitation.* Washington, DC: National Association of Housing and Redevelopment Officials.

Levy, P.R. 1978. *Queen Village: The Eclipse of Community.* Philadelphia, PA: Institute for the Study of Civic Values.

Levy, P.R. 1979. "Unloading the Neighborhood Bandwagon," *Social Policy* 10,2: 28-32.

Levy, P.R. 1980. "Neighborhoods in a Race with Time: Local Strategies for Countering Displacement," pp. 302-317 in Laska and Spain (1980).

Levy, P.R. and R.A. Cybriwsky. 1980. "The Hidden Dimensions of Culture and Class: Philadelphia," pp. 138-155 in Laska and Spain (1980).

Levy, P. and D. McGrath. 1979. "Saving Cities For Whom?" *Social Policy* 10,3: 20-28.

Lewis, P.F. 1975a. *New Orleans: The Making of an Urban Landscape.* Cambridge, MA: Ballinger.

Lewis, P.F. 1975b. "To Revive Urban Downtowns, Show Respect for the Spirit of the Place," *Smithsonian* 6,6:32-41.

Ley, D. 1980. "Liberal Ideology and the Post-industrial City," *Annals,* Association of American Geographers 70: 238-258.

Ley, D. 1981. "Inner City Revitalization in Canada: A Vancouver Case Study," *The Canadian Geographer* 25: 124-148.

Ley, D. and J. Mercer. 1980. "Locational Conflict and the Politics of Consumption," *Economic Geography* 56: 89-109.

Lineberry, R.L. 1977. *Equality and Urban Policy: The Distribution of Municipal Public Services.* Beverly Hills, CA: Sage.

Lipton, G.S. 1980. "Evidence of Central City Revival," pp. 42-60 in Laska and Spain (1980).

London, B. 1979. *The Revitalization of Inner City Neighborhoods: An Updated Bibliography.* Monticello, IL: Vance Bibliographies.

London, B. 1980. "Gentrification as Urban Reinvasion," pp. 77-92 in Laska and Spain (1980).

Long, L.H. 1980. "Back to the Countryside and Back to the City in the Same Decade," pp. 61-76 in Laska and Spain (1980).

Lowenthal, David. 1979. "Age and Artifact: Dilemmas of Appreciation," pp. 103-128 in D.W. Meinig (editor), *Interpretations of Ordinary Landscapes.* New York: Oxford University Press.

Lowry, I. 1960. "Filtering and Housing Standards," *Land Economics* 36: 362-370.

Lubove, R. 1962. *The Progressives and the Slums.* Pittsburgh, PA: University of Pittsburgh Press.

Lupo, A., F. Colcord, and E.P. Fowler. 1971. *Rites of Way.* Boston, MA: Little, Brown.

Marcuse, P. 1979. "The Deceptive Consensus on Redlining: Definitions Do Matter," *Journal of the American Planning Association* 45: 549-556.

Marris, P. 1974. *Loss and Change.* New York: Pantheon.

Mellor, R. 1975. "Urban Sociology in an Urbanized Society," *British Journal of Sociology* 26: 276-293.

Melman, S. 1977. "The Federal Rip-Off of New York's Money," pp. 181-188 in Alcaly and Mermelstein (1977).

Meek, C. 1978. "Public Displacement from 1952-1977," United States Department of Housing and Urban Development, Office of Community Planning and Development, *Working Paper.*

Meyer, K.E. 1979. "Love Thy City: Marketing the American Metropolis," *Saturday Review* 8 (April 28): 16-20.

Meyerson, M. and E.C. Banfield. 1955. *Politics, Planning and the Public Interest.* New York: The Free Press.

Milan, L.G. 1976. "Harrisburg Rebuilds Downtown Through Successful Leveraging of Public Funds," *Journal of Housing* 33: 482-485.

Mollenkopf, J.H. 1978. "The Postwar Politics of Urban Development," p. 117-152 in Tabb and Sawers (1978).

Molotch, H. 1976. "The City as a Growth Machine: Toward a Political Economy of Place," *American Journal of Sociology* 82: 309-332.

Moore, B. Jr. 1973. *Reflections on the Causes of Human Misery.* Boston, MA: Beacon Press.

Myers, P. 1978. *Neighborhood Conservation and the Elderly.* Washington, DC: The Conservation Foundation.

National Commission on Neighborhoods. 1979. *People, Building Neighborhoods.* Washington, DC: Government Printing Office.

National Trust for Historic Preservation. 1976. *Economic Benefits of Preserving Old Buildings.* Washington, DC: The Preservation Press.

Neighborhood Reinvestment Corporation. *No Date.* *A Partnership Approach to Neighborhood Commercial Reinvestment.* Washington, DC: Comptroller of the Currency.

Neighborhood Reinvestment Corporation. 1980. *A Common Ground: Neighborhood Partnerships.* Washington, DC: Comptroller of the Currency.

National Urban Coalition. 1978. *Displacement: City Neighborhoods in Transition.* Washington, DC: National Urban Coalition.

Nenno, M.K. 1980. "Community Development Block Grants: An Overview of the First Five Years," *Journal of Housing* 37: 435-442.

Newsom, M.D. 1971. "Blacks and Historic Preservation," *Law and Contemporary Problems* 36: 423-431.

New York City, Office of Economic Development. *No Date.* *Neighborhood Programs in Commercial Revitalization.* Unpublished document.

***New York Times* 1980.** "Revitalization Held to be Spotty," *The New York Times* (June 1): 8-1,8.

O'Loughlin, J. and D.C. Munski. 1979. "Housing Rehabilitation in the Inner City: A Comparison of Two Neighborhoods in New Orleans," *Economic Geography* 55: 52-70.

Owen, J.G. 1980. "A Sense of Place," *BEE, Bulletin of Environmental Education* (August-September).

Park, R.E., E.W. Burgess, and R.D. McKenzie (editors). 1925. *The City.* Chicago, IL: University of Chicago Press.

Pattison, T. 1977. *The Process of Neighborhood Upgrading and Gentrification.* Cambridge, MA: Massachusetts Institute of Technology, Department of Urban Studies and Planning, unpublished M.A. thesis.

Peet, R. (editor). 1977a. *Radical Geography.* Chicago, IL: Maaroufa.

Peet, R. 1977b. "The Development of Radical Geography in the United States," *Progress in Human Geography,* 1,3: 64-87.

Peirce, N.R. 1975. "Inequality and Poverty: A Marxist-Geographic Theory," *Annals, Association of American Geographers,* 65: 564-571.

Peirce, N.R. 1977. "Nation's Cities Poised for a Stunning Comeback," *The Washington Post* (July 3).

Perez, D., J.S. Garza, and B. Fulco. 1980. "Displacement: Hispanic Style," *Urban Concerns* 1,2: 52-54.

Perlman, J.E. 1976. "Grassrooting the System," *Social Policy* 7,2: 4-20.

Peterson, J.A. 1976. "The City Beautiful Movement: Forgotten Origins and Lost Meanings," *Journal of Urban History* 2,4: 415-434.

Pocock, D. and R. Hudson. 1978. *Images of The Urban Environment.* New York: Columbia University Press.

Policinski, G. 1978. "Indianapolis Outgrows Its Smalltown Image," *Planning* 44,4: 13-15.

Porteous, J.D. 1977. *Environment and Behavior.* Reading, MA: Addison-Wesley.

Prattner, J. and P.F. Mittelstadt. 1973. "St. Louis Inner-City Neighborhood Reclaiming Itself Through Community Development Corporation," *Journal of Housing* 30: 484-490.

President's Commission for a National Agenda for the Eighties. 1980. *Urban America in the Eighties.* Washington, DC: Government Printing Office.

Procter, M. and B. Matuszeski. 1978. *Gritty Cities.* Philadelphia, PA: Temple University Press.

Quayle, V. 1980. "Interview: Displacement in Baltimore," *Urban Concerns* 1,2: 42-45.

Rainwater, L. 1970. *Behind Ghetto Walls.* Chicago, IL: Aldine.

Redstone, L.G. 1976. *The New Downtowns.* New York: McGraw-Hill.

Rein, M. 1976. *Social Science and Public Policy.* New York: Penguin.

Relph, E. 1976. *Place and Placelessness.* London: Pion.

Relph, E. 1981. "Phenomenology," pp. 99-114 in M.E. Harvey and B.P. Holly (editors), *Themes in Geographic Thought.* New York: St. Martin's.

Reuss, M. 1979. "Local Solutions for Local Problems: Economic Development for the Neighborhoods," Vol. 4, pp. 72-87 in Hines *et al.* (1979).

Richards, C. and J. Rowe. 1977. "Restoring a City: Who Pays the Price?" *Working Papers For A New Society* 4,4: 54-61.

Rifkind, C. 1977. *Main Street: The Face of Urban America.* New York: Harper and Row.

Rosenfeld, R.A. 1980. "Who Benefits and Who Decides? The Uses of Community Development Block Grants," pp. 211-235 in Rosenthal (1980).

Rosenthal, D.B. (editor). 1980. *Urban Revitalization.* Beverly Hills, CA: Sage.

Roweis, S.T. and A.J. Scott. 1978. "The Urban Land Question," pp. 38-75 in Cox (1978).

Rubin, B. 1979. "Aesthetic Ideology and Urban Design," *Annals,* Association of American Geographers 69: 339-361.

Rule, J.B. 1978. *Insight and Social Betterment.* New York: Oxford University Press.

Saarinen, T. 1976. *Environmental Planning: Perception and Behavior.* Boston, MA: Houghton Mifflin.

Sale, K. 1977. "Six Pillars of the Southern Rim," pp. 165-180 in Alcaly and Mermelstein (1977).

Sanders, H.T. 1980. "Urban Renewal and the Revitalized City: A Reconsideration of Recent History," pp. 103-126 in Rosenthal (1980).

Sands, S.M. 1979. *Population Change Due to Housing Renovation in St. Paul's Ramsey Hill Area.* St. Paul, MN: University of Minnesota, unpublished M.A. thesis.

Sawers, L. 1975. "Urban Form and the Mode of Production," *Review of Radical Political Economics* 7,1: 52-68.

Schoenberg, S.P. and P.L. Rosenbaum. 1980. *Neighborhoods That Work.* New Brunswick, NJ: Rutgers University Press.

Schultz, C.L. "_ +Y¡ **1977.** "Fiscal Problems of Cities," pp. 189-212 in Alcaly and Mermelstein (1977).

Scott, M. 1969. *American City Planning.* Berkeley, CA: University of California Press.

Seline, W.G. 1976. "Tax Increment Financing: A Key Preservation Tool," pp. 49-50 in National Trust for Historic Preservation (1976).

Sherrin, W. 1980. "Detroiters Confronting a Choice: New Jobs or Old Neighborhoods," *The New York Times* (September 15).

Slater, D. 1977. "The Poverty of Modern Geographical Enquiry." pp. 40-57 in Peet (1977a).

Smith, D.M. 1977. *Human Geography: A Welfare Approach.* New York: St. Martin's.

Smith, D.M. 1979. *Geographic Perspectives on Inequality.* New York: Barnes and Noble.

Smith, M. P. 1979. *The City and Social Theory.* New York: St. Martin's.

Smith, N. 1979a. "Gentrification and Capital: Theory, Practice and Ideology in Society Hill," *Antipode* 11,3: 24-35.

Smith, N. 1979b. "Toward a Theory of Gentrification: A Back to the City Movement by Capital not People," *Journal of the American Planning Association* 45: 538-548.

Smith, N. 1981. "Gentrification and Uneven Development," Presented at conference on New Perspectives on the Urban Political Economy, Washington, DC.

Smith, P.F. 1973. "Symbolic Meaning in Contemporary Cities," *RIBJA* 80: 436-441.

Smith, W.F. 1971. "Filtering and Neighborhood Change," pp. 170-179 in L.S. Bourne (editor), *Internal Structure of the City.* New York: Oxford University Press.

Socialist Geographers' Specialty Group. 1981. *Workshop on Community, Redevelopment, Response.* Presented at the Annual Meeting of Association of American Geographers, Los Angeles.

Soja, E.W. 1980. "The Socio-Spatial Dialectic," *Annals,* Association of American Geographers 70: 207-225.

Spain, D. 1980. "Indicators of Urban Revitalization: Racial and Socioeconomic Changes in Central City Housing," pp. 27-41 in Laska and Spain (1980).

Squires, G.D. "_ +Yᵢ **1979.** "Urban Decline or Disinvestment," *Social Problems* 27: 79-95.

Starr, R. 1978. "Making New York Smaller," pp. 378-389 in Sternlieb and Hughes (1978).

Sternlieb, G. and J.W. Hughes (editors). 1975. *Post-Industrial America.* New Brunswick, NJ: Center for Urban Policy Research.

Sternlieb, G. and J.W. Hughes (editors). 1978. *Revitalizing the Northeast.* New Brunswick, NJ: Center for Urban Policy Research.

Sternlieb, G. and J.W. Hughes. 1979a. "Back to the Central City: Myths and Realities," *Traffic Quarterly* 33: 617-636.

Sternlieb, G. and J.W. Hughes. 1979b. "New Dimensions of the Urban Crisis." Paper prepared for the Subcommittee on Fiscal and Intergovernmental Policy, Joint Economic Committee of Congress of the United States.

Stoddart, D.R. (editor). 1981. *Geography, Ideology and Social Concerns.* New York: Barnes and Noble.

Stone, C.N. 1976. *Economic Growth and Neighborhood Discontent.* Chapel Hill, NC: University of North Carolina Press.

Stout, G. and O. Otteson. 1980. "Neighborhood Commercial Revitalization in St. Paul," *Challenge* 11,2: 10-14.

Straus, N. 1945. *The Seven Myths of Housing.* New York: Alfred A. Knopf.

Subcommittee on Capital, Investment and Business Opportunities, House of Representatives. 1978. *Neighborhood Business District Revitalization.* Washington, DC: Government Printing Office.

Subcommittee on the City. 1977. *Toward a National Urban Policy.* Washington, DC: Government Printing Office.

Sumka, H. 1979. "Neighborhood Revitalization and Displacement: A Review of the Evidence," *Journal of the American Planning Association* 45: 480-487.

Sumka, H. 1980a. "Federal Antidisplacement Policy in a Context of Urban Decline," pp. 269-287 in Laska and Spain (1980).

Sumka, H. 1980b. "Is Residential Displacement a Critical Urban Problem? — Con," *Urban Concerns* 1,2: 31-40.

Sutton, C. 1980. "Creative Financing Gives Long Beach a Head Start," *Planning* 46,8: 12-15.

Sutton, H. 1979. "The Comeback of Downtown — America Falls in Love with its Cities — Again," *Saturday Review* 6 (July 5): 16-21.

Tabb, W.K. 1978. "The New York City Fiscal Crisis," 241-266 in Tabb and Sawers (1978).

Tabb, W.K. and L. Sawers (editors) 1978. *Marxism and the Metropolis.* New York: Oxford University Press.

Thurow, L.C. 1980. *The Zero-Sum Society.* New York: Penguin.

Time. **1976.** "Downtown is Looking Up," *Time* 113 (July 5): 60-67.

Toll, S.I. 1969. *Zoned America.* New York: Grossman.

Tournier, R. 1980. "Historic Preservation as a Force in Urban Change: Charleston," pp. 173-86 in Laska and Spain (1980).

Tuan, Y. 1974. *Topophilia.* Englewood Cliffs, NJ: Prentice-Hall.

Tuan, Y. 1977. *Space and Place: The Perspective of Experience.* Minneapolis, MN: University of Minnesota Press.

Tuan, Y. 1979. *Landscapes of Fear.* New York: Pantheon.

Uhlman, W. 1976. "Economics Aside," pp. 5-7 in National Trust for Historic Preservation (1976).

U.S. Bureau of the Census. 1975. *Historical Statistics of the United States, Colonial Times to 1970.* Washington, DC: Government Printing Office.

U.S. Department of Housing and Urban Development. 1975. *Urban Renewal Directory, June 30, 1974.* Washington, DC: Government Printing Office.

U.S. Dept. HUD. 1978. *The President's National Urban Policy Report.* Washington, DC: Government Printing Office.

U.S. Dept. HUD. 1979a. *The Impact of Foreign Direct Investments on U.S. Cities and Regions.* Washington, DC: Government Printing Office.

U.S. Dept. HUD. 1979b. *Neighborhoods: A Self-Help Sampler.* Washington, DC: Government Printing Office.

U.S. Dept. HUD. 1980. *Commercial Revitalization – Neighborhood Focus.* Washington, DC: Government Printing Office.

U.S. Department of Labor. 1976. *Employment and Training Report of the President.* Washington, D.C.: Government Printing Office.

U.S. Federal Works Agency. 1942. *Final Statistical Report of the Federal Emergency Relief Administration.* Washington, DC: Government Printing Office.

U.S. Public Works Administration. 1939. *America Builds: The Record of PWA.* Washington, DC: Government Printing Office.

Volsky, G. 1981. "Condominium Conversions Tied to Stress in Elderly," *The New York Times* (May 31): 47.

Wagner, P. 1972. *Environments and Peoples.* Englewood Cliffs, NJ: Prentice-Hall.

Waterstone, M. and B. Holcomb. 1981. "Waterfront Revitalization: Diluting a Resource." Paper presented at the Annual Meeting of the Middle States Division of the Association of American Geographers, Rochester, NY.

Weiler, C. 1978. *Reinvestment Displacement: HUD's Role in a New Housing Issue.* Report prepared for the Office of Community Planning and Development, U.S. Department of Housing and Urban Development.

Weiler, C. 1980. "The Neighborhood's Role in Optimizing Reinvestment: Philadelphia," pp. 220-235 in Laska and Spain (1980).

White, G. 1972. "Geography and Public Policy," *The Professional Geographer* 24: 101-104.

Williams, J.T. 1978. "Neighborhood Development In Providence (R.I.)," *Challenge* 9,3: 18-21.

Williams, R.M. 1977. "Facelift for Detroit," *Saturday Review* 4 (May 14): 6-11.

Wilson, W.H. 1964. *The City Beautiful Movement in Kansas City.* Columbia, MO: University of Missouri Press.

Winsberg, M.D. 1980. "The Changing Concentration of U.S. Industrial Employment, 1940-1977," *Journal of Geography* 79,4: 144-148.

Winters, C. 1979. "The Social Identity of Evolving Neighborhoods," *Landscape* 23,1: 8-14.

Wood, E.E. 1935. *Slums and Blighted Areas in the United States.* Washington, DC: Federal Emergency Administration of Public Works, Housing Division, *Bulletin* No. 1.

Worthy, W. 1976. *The Rape of Our Neighborhoods.* New York: William Morrow.

Zambo, P.W. 1975. "Allentown, Pennsylvania Halts Central City Cycle of 'Deterioration, Decay and Abandonment,' " *Journal of Housing* 32: 233-236.

Zeitz, E. 1979. *Private Urban Renewal.* Lexington, MA: D.C. Heath.